Apple® Vision Pro™

by Marc Saltzman

Apple® Vision Pro™ For Dummies®

Published by: **John Wiley & Sons, Inc.,** 111 River Street, Hoboken, NJ 07030-5774, www.wiley.com

For general information on our other products and services, please contact our Customer Care Department within the U.S. at 877-762-2974, outside the U.S. at 317-572-3993, or fax 317-572-4002. For technical support, please visit https://hub.wiley.com/community/support/dummies.

Wiley publishes in a variety of print and electronic formats and by print-on-demand. Some material included with standard print versions of this book may not be included in e-books or in print-on-demand. If this book refers to media that is not included in the version you purchased, you may download this material at http://booksupport.wiley.com. For more information about Wiley products, visit www.wiley.com.

Library of Congress Control Number: 2024943817

ISBN 978-1-394-27990-6 (pbk); ISBN 978-1-394-27992-0 (ebk); ISBN 978-1-394-27991-3 (ebk)

SKY10086285_100124

Apple® Vision Pro™

for dummies®
A Wiley Brand

Contents at a Glance

Table of Contents

Introduction

Welcome, friend, to the ultimate guide for using — nay, mastering — your Apple Vision Pro! Apple's latest gadget is so different, and can do so much, that I'd argue you *need* a plain-English resource like this to get the most out of it.

For real. This thing is crazy. You're literally using your eyes, voice, and gestures in the air to control content — not unlike Tom Cruise's character, Chief John Anderton, in the sci-fi film *Minority Report*. As a result, without this book, Apple Vision Pro could be overwhelming.

Left to your own devices — pun intended — you may not fully take advantage of what the futuristic Apple Vision Pro is capable of. For this reason, I felt compelled to take everything this wearable headset can do and explain it in a way that anyone can understand.

What you're holding is the definitive companion to Apple Vision Pro — but it's much more than just an instruction manual.

About This Book

At a high level, this book explains how to take full advantage of the Apple Vision Pro, as well as its interface, features, and apps. Like all *For Dummies* books, this book is a straightforward and easy-to-follow handbook. I've organized it in parts that make sense and populate each part with related chapters that explore the many aspects of Apple Vision Pro.

Aside from a teeny booklet, Apple Vision Pro doesn't include any information to get going, so consider *Apple Vision Pro For Dummies* the closest thing to an instruction manual — and a whole lot more. Like an instruction manual, you don't have to read it from beginning to end or commit it to memory — there will no test at the end of the week. Instead, you can turn to it whenever you're looking for information on how to use your Apple Vision Pro.

If you're short on time, you can safely skip *sidebars* (text in gray boxes), as well as anything marked with the Technical Stuff icon (more on that later in this Introduction).

Keep in mind that Apple adds new features to its devices over time, or may remove or tweak a setting or app, so you may need to do a little experimentation on your own if things aren't exactly the way I describe them in this book. Don't fret — you can't wreck your (expensive!) Apple Vision Pro by clicking the wrong thing.

Within this book, you may note that some web addresses break across two lines of text. If you're reading this book in print and want to visit one of these web pages, simply key in the web address exactly as it's noted in the text, pretending as though the line break doesn't exist. If you're reading this as an e-book, you've got it easy — just click the web address to be taken directly to the web page.

Finally, while writing this book, I consulted Apple's official online documentation on the Apple Vision Pro. When I quote directly from Apple's documentation, I note that.

Foolish Assumptions

When writing this book, I made only two major assumptions:

» You own Apple Vision Pro or are about to.

» You want to know how to get the most out of it.

Icons Used in This Book

The following icons are placed in the margins of the book's pages to point out information you may or may not want to read.

TIP

The Tip icon offers suggestions to enhance your experience with Apple Vision Pro.

REMEMBER

The Remember icon highlights anything worth committing to memory. You might consider bookmarking the page or jotting down the information elsewhere.

WARNING

Apple Vision Pro is a promising new wearable platform, but the Warning icon alerts you to important considerations when using it, including health, safety, or security concerns.

TECHNICAL STUFF

The Technical Stuff icon warns you about geeky descriptions or explanations you may want to pass on — but don't expect a lot of these throughout this easy-to-read guide.

Beyond This Book

In addition to the information in this book, you get access to even more help and information online at Dummies.com. Check out this book's online Cheat Sheet for tips on mastering the gestures in Apple Vision Pro, getting the most out of the headset, and capturing incredibly immersive spatial photos and videos. Just go to www.dummies.com and type **Apple Vision Pro For Dummies Cheat Sheet** in the Search box.

Where to Go from Here

If you have Apple Vision Pro, it's time to take it out of the box, power it up, and get ready to use it for the first time. You can dive into the book whenever you're good to go.

There's nothing else you need to know before flipping through *Apple Vision Pro For Dummies.* I'm ready when you are, so turn the page and get started!

1

Getting Started with Apple Vision Pro

Understand what makes Apple Vision Pro unique, and get an overview of all the extraordinary things you can do with it.

Learn all the parts to Apple Vision Pro and successfully set up the headset for the first time.

Explore the many ways you can interact with Apple Vision Pro — using your hands, eyes, and voice — and find out how to navigate through apps and other content.

Get to know the Home View, Environment, App Store, and included apps, as well as optional Accessibility settings.

Set up your own unique Persona, a digital representation of yourself, for use with FaceTime video calls and SharePlay-supported apps and games.

Chapter **1**

Getting to Know Apple Vision Pro

A pple Vision Pro is the most exciting new Apple product in years — perhaps decades. And it's easily the most ambitious. Apple Vison Pro may be difficult to explain — especially if you haven't played around with any other headsets that came before it — but you've come to the right place.

In this chapter, I introduce you to the Apple Vision Pro — covering everything from what it is and what it does to how it differs from other headsets and what it can do for you. If you're curious about Apple Vision Pro, or if you have one and you don't know where to start, this chapter (and book!) is for you.

Virtual Reality and Augmented Reality: It All Comes Together in Apple Vision Pro

Apple refers to Apple Vision Pro as a "spatial computer," but it's really a high-tech headset that fuses virtual reality with augmented reality to create mixed reality:

>> **Virtual reality (VR):** In VR, you put on a special headset and you're engaged with a fully immersive digital environment. You don't see the real world through the headset — you only see a virtual world, and it's super immersive because the visuals are all around you, in 360 degrees. What you see is also tied to head tracking, which means wherever you turn your head while wearing the headset — up, down, side to side, or even behind you — that same perspective is seen in the virtual world you're in. Because of this feature, VR can trick your brain into thinking that what you're seeing is the real deal.

But it doesn't just stop there. Audio is also "spatialized" in a VR world, so you can hear sounds all around you, such as a moaning zombie creeping up from behind you, a towering dinosaur in front of you, or someone talking to you from the right or left of you. The audio helps add to the effect.

>> **Augmented reality (AR):** In AR, you can still see the real world around you — either through a headset you wear or by holding up your smartphone and looking through the camera lens — but what you see is *augmented* (enhanced) with digital information.

The hit mobile game Pokémon GO is an example of AR. You hold up your phone at, say, a park, and you see the real-world trees, bushes, and park benches on your phone's screen — but superimposed on top are cute Pokémon creatures, so it looks like they're right there with you.

Wearing a headset with AR works the same way, but it's even cooler because you're hands-free.

So, where does Apple Vision Pro fit into all this? It seamlessly blends AR and VR into one device to create a mixed reality (MR) experience, allowing you to toggle between AR and VR, depending on the application and/or your environment while wearing what looks like futuristic ski goggles (see Figure 1-1). So, you can stay "present" with what's going on around you in the real world, or you can completely close yourself off from your surroundings.

For example, you may be video chatting with someone online over FaceTime, but you're still able to pour dog food into a bowl and serve it to your furry friend doing the dinnertime dance at your feet. This feature is often referred to as *passthrough*, because you can see the real world when you want to.

FIGURE 1-1:
The Apple
Vision Pro
headset.

Courtesy of Apple, Inc.

Alternatively, if you're alone on the sofa and you want to kick back and watch a movie, Apple Vision Pro will automatically dim the family room so you see only the giant (virtual) video screen in front of you. Or you can choose to engage in a VR experience like Encounter Dinosaurs, where you come face-to-face with the prehistoric beasts, and you're completely immersed in the experience (see Figure 1-2). You can even "interact" with the dinosaurs — try to touch different creatures, and they'll likely respond differently. Plus, if you move around during the experience, the dinosaurs' eyes will follow your movements. Turn to Chapter 9 for more on Encounter Dinosaurs.

FIGURE 1-2:
Encounter
Dinosaurs
brings
dinosaurs into
your living
room . . . if
you dare!

Courtesy of Apple, Inc.

REMEMBER

Other headsets, such as the Meta Quest 3, can straddle AR and VR and have passthrough. Part of what makes Apple Vision Pro unique is *how* you access the content (see the next section).

The Apple Vision Pro User Interface: Using Your Eyes, Hands, and Voice

Instead of using videogame-like controllers, you control three-dimensional user interface of Apple Vision Pro using your eyes, hands, and voice. You highlight an app or image merely by looking at it; reach into the air to "touch" (select) the digital content or "pin" it to one side of the room you're in; use gestures (see Figure 1-3) to swipe up, down, and side to side to navigate through virtual items (say, while inside a game or photo library); and summon Siri, your voice-activated personal assistant, as yet another way to interact with it all. (Turn to Chapter 3 for much more detail about how to use the Apple Vision Pro controls and Chapter 5 to tweak Apple Vision Pro settings.)

FIGURE 1-3: You can access content with gestures, as well as eye movement and your voice.

Courtesy of Apple, Inc.

TECHNICAL STUFF

In all fairness, Microsoft paved the way for Apple Vision Pro with its HoloLens mixed-reality headset, which debuted in 2016. Although primarily used for business applications, HoloLens introduced many of these gesture-based controls popularized by Apple today.

You can also add a wireless Magic Keyboard and/or Magic Trackpad, if you want to treat Apple Vision Pro like an extension of your Mac experience.

TIP

If you haven't ordered Apple Vision Pro yet, be aware that you must scan your face using an iPhone or iPad with Face ID for fitting purposes. It's similar to setting up Face ID to log into your iPhone, iPad, or Mac. If you can't do this or don't want to do it, you can do a facial scan at your local Apple Store, with the help of a staff member.

LIVING IN THE APPLE UNIVERSE

A key differentiator between Apple Vision Pro and other headsets is that only Apple Vision Pro can run popular Apple apps you may already use on your iPhone, iPad, and Mac. This includes default apps like App Store, Books, Calendar, Camera, Contacts, FaceTime, Files, Keynote, Mail, Maps, Messages, Mindfulness, Music, News, Notes, Photos, Reminders, Safari, Stocks, Voice Memos, and more — all in mixed reality. Check out the figure — don't these apps look familiar?

Courtesy of Apple, Inc.

Plus, because most of these apps are synchronized over iCloud, when you log into, say, Photos or Notes, what you see in Apple Vision Pro is the same as what you see on your other Apple devices (and vice versa).

Apple Vision Pro is powered by Apple's visionOS, billed by Apple as the "world's first spatial operating system" (though Microsoft and the HoloLens team may have something to say about that!). visionOS now joins other Apple operating systems: iOS (for iPhone), iPadOS (for iPad), macOS (for Mac computers), watchOS (for Apple Watch), and tvOS (for Apple TV).

Finding Out What's in the Box

When you open the Apple Vision Pro box for the first time, here's what you'll find inside:

- » Apple Vision Pro headset with cover
- » Battery with attached power cable
- » 30W USB-C power adapter
- » USB-C charge cable
- » Light Seal
- » Two Light Seal Cushions
- » Solo Knit Band
- » Dual Loop Band
- » Enclosure and audio straps
- » Polishing cloth
- » Information booklet

Before you can begin using Apple Vision Pro, you'll need to charge the battery, connect the power cable, and attach your ZEISS Optical Inserts (if you use them). Sold by Apple and developed in partnership with ZEISS, custom optical inserts are supported for users with prescription glasses; the optical inserts magnetically attach to the main lens inside the headset (see Figure 1-4).

TIP

Apple also sells other accessories for Apple Vision Pro, including the Apple Vision Pro Travel Case ($199), Light Seal ($199), and Light Seal Cushion ($29). For developers, there's also the Developer Strap for Vision Pro ($299), which includes a dongle to connect the headset to a PC or Mac via a USB-C cable, which helps with creating and transferring large apps, games, and files. At the time of this writing, the only official third-party accessory available is a battery holder made by Belkin.

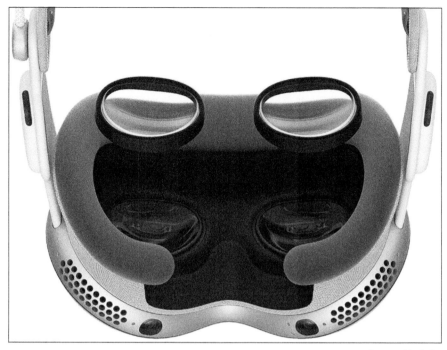

FIGURE 1-4:
ZEISS Optical
Inserts allow
people who
wear glasses
to use Apple
Vision Pro.

Courtesy of Apple, Inc.

Covering the Apple Vision Pro Specs

After you remove the soft cushion cover from your Apple Vision Pro, you'll see it has a smooth, curved laminated glass display on the front and a flexible cushion, called a Light Seal, on the inside surrounding the two 1.41-inch micro LED displays (one for each eye), as shown in Figure 1-5. The Light Seal connects magnetically to the inside of the visor.

The twin 4K screens (3,660 x 3,200 pixels each) displays a total of 23 megapixels, running at a smooth 90 frames per second (but depending on the content, it could automatically increase to 96 or 100 frames per second). Also on the front of the headset are five sensors, six microphones, and 12 cameras.

The cameras and sensors allow you to see the room you're in. They're also used to capture amazingly realistic photos and videos (see Chapter 13). Infrared cameras and sensors (accelerometers and gyroscopes) read your face, too. They use iris-tracking technology (so Apple Vision Pro knows where you're looking on the screen), mirror your real-time facial expressions in a FaceTime call (see Chapter 6), and much more.

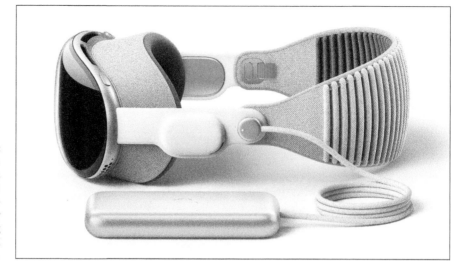

FIGURE 1-5:
Apple Vision Pro with its dark visor and Light Seal (the mesh gray part) covering the twin 4K screens.

TECHNICAL STUFF

An *accelerometer* is a sensor that measures acceleration, which is a change in speed or direction. Similarly, a *gyroscope* is used for rotational tracking in a three-dimensional space (sensing movements of pitch, yaw, and roll). In a device like a smartphone or headset, the accelerometer and gyroscope work together to provide more complete and accurate movement tracking.

As you set up your Apple Vision Pro for the first time, your face will be scanned by the headset (see Figure 1-6) to generate a *Persona* (a realistic-looking avatar of yourself to use in FaceTime calls and other applications).

FIGURE 1-6:
You'll scan your face in Apple Vision Pro and use this Persona to video chat with others online, among other things.

An Apple Vision Pro feature called EyeSight shows the eyes of your avatar through your Apple Vision Pro headset, which appear dimmed when in AR apps or opaque when in full VR immersion. When someone approaches you and/or speaks, EyeSight shows their Persona's virtual eyes normally, and the person is visible to you. (Turn to Chapter 2 for more information.)

The headset has an aluminum frame on its sides, a removable and adjustable headband, and the Digital Crown (a twistable knob) on the right side of Apple Vision Pro to tighten or loosen the fit.

For audio, Apple Vision Pro has a bone conduction speaker inside the headband, which is placed directly over each of your ears and supports surround sound. At any time, you can add Bluetooth wireless headphones or earbuds, too, if you want.

Twin cooling fans (about 1.6 inches in diameter) are near the eyes to help dispense heat, and noise-canceling technology makes it so you don't hear the fans.

Apple Vision Pro is powered by the M2 chip. The M2 is custom Apple-made silicon, with a unique dual-chip design. It's accompanied by a co-processor referred to as Apple R1, used primarily for real-time sensor input processing.

As for storage, when you buy Apple Vision Pro, you'll need to choose from one of three options: 256GB, 512GB, and 1TB. You can't upgrade the storage in the future, so be sure to order a device with enough storage to suit your needs. I recommend at least 512GB, so you don't have buyer's remorse if you run out of room on your headset. If you want to download a lot of games and apps (dozens of them), or you want to view many and/or longer videos, go for 1TB of storage — budget permitting, of course.

Unfortunately, the Apple Vision Pro battery isn't built into the headset itself. Instead, Apple Vision Pro is powered by an external battery about the size of an iPhone. It looks like a silver power bank you may have to charge up your iPhone when you're out and about. The silver lining, at least, is that if the battery needs to be replaced for any reason, you're not without your entire headset (plus, you can buy a second, backup battery and swap it out easily, if you're not going to be near a power outlet for a while). The headset has a small port on the right side that connects to the white USB-C cable, which plugs into the power supply. According to Apple, you can also attach Apple Vision Pro to a USB-C port on a Mac or another power bank battery rated for at least two and a half hours of use.

Chapter **2**

Setting Up Apple Vision Pro

You got your shiny new Apple Vision Pro, and you're eager to get going with it. I can't blame you. In this chapter, I cover the basics of Apple Vision Pro, such as charging the battery, securing a snug fit, and setting up the headset for the first time. I also share some maintenance tips to ensure it runs smoothly for years to come.

Charging and Connecting the Battery

Before you can get started with Apple Vision Pro, you need to charge the battery by plugging it into the wall with the included USB-C cable and power adapter. (You don't need to connect the battery to the headset yet, unless you want to.) The light on the battery will turn from orange to green when it's fully charged.

TIP

If you're thinking, "Hey, can't I just plug the battery into my MacBook to charge it?" you *can*, but it'll take longer than plugging it into an AC outlet.

After the battery is charged, follow these steps to connect the battery to Apple Vision Pro:

1. **Put the battery in a secure place nearby, such as in front of you on a table or in your pocket.**

2. **Align and insert the power cable into the power connector — on the left side of the headset, right where the headset connects to the Solo Knit Band — and make sure that the cable is pointing upward, so the LED aligns with the open dot.**

3. **Turn on Apple Vision Pro by rotating the power cable clockwise, aligning the LED with the solid dot to lock in the cable (see Figure 2-1).**

   The white LED begins pulsing. When you hear a tone, the device is ready to wear.

   If you connect the battery and you don't hear a tone after 30 to 45 seconds, press and hold the top-left button on the headset for a few seconds to turn on Apple Vision Pro.

4. **If you're using ZEISS Optical Inserts, attach them to Apple Vision Pro.**

   Refer to the ZEISS Optical Inserts package for instructions.

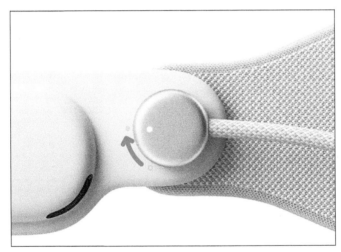

FIGURE 2-1:
Turn on Apple Vision Pro by rotating the power cable clockwise, aligning the LED with the solid dot.

Courtesy of Apple, Inc.

WARNING

If you want to disconnect the battery from Apple Vision Pro, be sure to first save any open documents or notes or whatever else you're working on because disconnecting the battery will turn off the device. To disconnect the battery from the headset, turn the power cable counterclockwise until the cable detaches.

TIP

Even when you're *not* using Apple Vision Pro, it's a good idea to always leave the portable battery connected so the headset can synchronize your mail, photos, and more. (Just make sure if the headset is safe from damage. If it's on a table, for example, make sure the battery is on the table, too — a dangling battery could accidentally pull the headset off a ledge, resulting in a costly accident. It's best to put the headset and connected battery back in the box or a carrying case.)

And be aware that, in order to preserve battery power, Apple Vision Pro will automatically shut down after 24 hours of inactivity, unless it's charging up.

Putting on the Headset

If you haven't done so already, remove the protective cloth from the front of Apple Vision Pro before you put it on. Then gently pull back the Solo Knit Band and position Apple Vision Pro on your face. Hold Apple Vision Pro securely with one hand, slide the headband over the back of your head, and adjust until secure by twisting the Fit Dial on the right side of the band. It should feel snug, but not too tight. Figure 2-2 shows how it should look when secured over your head.

FIGURE 2-2:
An essential
fit is key to
your Apple
Vision Pro
experience.

Courtesy of Apple, Inc.

TIP

The headset will display a message to you if it's too low or too high on your face, so you can make a quick adjustment.

REMEMBER

Apple Vision Pro is designed with a range of ways to customize fit — you're not limited to using the Fit Dial. To ensure a personalized fit, consider making some adjustments. For example, shift the Solo Knit Band and up and down until you feel equal support on your forehead and cheeks. Apple Vision Pro also comes with the Dual Loop Band, which is a great option if you want a fit that goes above and behind your head instead of only behind it (see Figure 2-3).

FIGURE 2-3:
If you don't like the way the Solo Knit Band fits, you can use the Dual Loop Band instead.

Courtesy of Apple, Inc.

To swap out the Solo Knit Band with the Dual Loop Band, follow these steps:

1. **Place your Apple Vision Pro on a stable surface with the visor cover on.**

2. **Pull the orange tabs to detach the Solo Knit Band.**

3. **Attach the Dual Loop Band with the upper strap oriented vertically.**

   The lower strap should be positioned so it goes around the back of your head. Push the connectors together until you hear a click.

4. **Loosen the upper and lower straps completely.**

5. **Hold Apple Vision Pro securely and place it over your head.**

6. Continue holding the device while firmly pressing the Light Seal cushion into your face with equal pressure on your forehead and cheeks.

7. While continuing to hold Apple Vision Pro in place, use your free hand to tighten the lower strap against the back of your head.

8. Use your free hand to tighten the upper strap snugly as well.

9. To fine-tune the fit, gently push up on Apple Vision Pro while pulling down on the lower strap until the position feels good to you.

Using Apple Vision Pro for the First Time

After you've adjusted the fit of Apple Vision Pro, you're ready to use it. You'll need Wi-Fi in order to properly set up Apple Vision Pro for first-time use.

TIP

Depending on where you live, you can get help with your Apple Vision Pro via a personal session with an Apple Specialist. After your new Apple Vision Pro ships, you'll receive an invitation to schedule your online session. (If you pick up your Apple Vision Pro at an Apple Store, you can opt to receive an email invitation for an online session.) Find out more at www.apple.com/shop/browse/overlay/vision/session or just search the web for "help Apple Vision Pro specialist."

The following sections walk you through the steps.

Step 1: Aligning your view

Start by placing Apple Vision Pro on your head. You'll be able to see not only your surroundings but also onscreen instructions. Apple Vision Pro will prompt you to press and hold the Digital Crown (see Figure 2-4) and stare directly ahead at the floating glasses in front of your eyes. This aligns your view.

Step 2: Signing in to your Apple ID

You have two options for signing in:

» **Quick Start:** If you own an iPhone (running iOS 17 or newer) or iPad (running iPadOS 17 or later), you can use Quick Start to automatically set up your Apple Vision Pro. Just bring your Apple Vision Pro and your iPhone or iPad close together, look at your iPhone or iPad, tap Continue, and follow the instructions. You will see a QR code to scan with the Apple Vision Pro to continue.

FIGURE 2-4:
A top-down view of Apple Vision Pro, showing the right side, where the Digital Crown button and dial is located (over your right eye).

Courtesy of Apple, Inc.

Your iPhone or iPad will share your Wi-Fi info to Apple Vision Pro and connect to your Apple ID (your email address associated with all things Apple). If desired, you can choose to manually enter your Apple ID credentials using a virtual keyboard floating in front of you.

REMEMBER

Children under 13 years of age can't sign in to Apple Vision Pro with their Apple IDs.

You will also need to also type in a six-digit multifactor authentication code from your iPhone or iPad to authorize it.

TECHNICAL STUFF

Multifactor authentication, sometimes referred to as *two-factor authentication,* is when you not only need a password to log into an account, but also need a one-time code sent to your mobile device that also needs to be entered to prove it's really you.

REMEMBER

You can see through the headset and look at your iPhone or iPad at the same time. You don't have to take off Apple Vision Pro to look at one of these devices.

» **Manual:** If you don't have an iPhone or iPad running the proper operating system, tap Set Up Manually. You can also choose this option if you don't want to carry over info from another device. It's entirely up to you. Simply follow along with the instructions inside the headset.

Step 3: Scanning your hands

Hand gestures are a big part of the Apple Vision Pro experience, so you have to show the device what your hands look like. You're prompted to stick your arms out in front of you and hold your hands up with their backs facing the headset (palms facing out). Then you're prompted to flip your hands over so your palms are facing your visor.

Step 4: Calibrating eye tracking

You're prompted to stare at a dot, then at six dots in a circle. You're instructed to make a tap gesture with your finger as you look at each dot. You'll go through a couple of rounds of this, with varying brightness, to see how your eyes look at objects when dilated.

Step 5: Setting up your Persona for FaceTime calls

Unlike FaceTime video calls on iPhone, iPad, and Mac, FaceTime on Apple Vision Pro relies on an avatar you need to create, called a *Persona*. Your Persona is a digital representation of you for things like FaceTime calls and other applications (see Chapter 6 for more). It's what others will see when you're chatting with them online. Your facial expressions and mouth movement will be mapped onto your Persona, so it looks like it's really you.

That is, unlike FaceTime on iPhone, iPad, and Mac, where your exact face is seen all the time by whoever you're interacting with (in 2D), in Apple Vision Pro it's a virtual and 3D version of yourself. Your real-time facial expressions and mouth movement are mapped onto your Persona, so it looks like it's really you.

To create your Persona, Apple Vision Pro cameras capture images and 3D measurements of your face, head, upper body, and facial expressions. The data is then used to build your Persona.

To set up your Persona, follow these steps:

1. **In the Settings app, tap Persona and then tap Get Started.**

2. **Refine your hand setup, and watch the tutorial video to learn the best practices to capture your Persona.**

   If you've watched the video before, you can tap Continue to skip it.

3. **When instructed, take off Apple Vision Pro, hold it carefully by the frame on each side of the headset, and turn it around so the front is facing you at eye level.**

4. **Follow the spoken instructions you'll hear through the headset.**

   The instructions prompt you to turn your head in different directions and make various expressions while you hold Apple Vision Pro in front of you (see Figure 2-5).

TIP

   The instructions are pretty loud, but if you aren't able to hear them, visuals on the front display also appear to guide you through the process:

   - **Directional arrows:** Slowly turn your head in the indicated direction.
   - **Four rings:** Smile with your mouth closed.
   - **Three rings:** Make a big smile with your teeth showing.
   - **Two rings:** Raise your eyebrows.
   - **One ring:** Close your eyes for a moment.
   - **No rings:** Put Apple Vision Pro back on.

FIGURE 2-5:
Apple Vision
Pro scans your
face to create
your Persona.

Courtesy of Apple, Inc.

TIP

To get a great Persona, check out these tips:

>> **Be aware of your room lighting.** Try to find a space with good lighting on your face, without shadows. On a related note, avoid bright overhead lighting

(it's just not very flattering) and bright light behind you (which can make you look dark, like a silhouette).

>> **When you capture your Persona, stand or sit in front of a neutral background (one that's not too busy).**

>> **Don't move around when you start scanning your face.** Stay in the same location, if you can, from start to finish.

>> **Relax your shoulders while holding Apple Vision Pro.** Apple says this will allow the cameras to better capture you naturally.

>> **Try to maintain a natural facial expression (not too forced) to best capture your genuine smile and other expressions.**

After you capture your Persona, you can edit it by adjusting the lighting, temperature, and brightness, or selecting a pair of glasses if that's what you wear in real life. (*Remember:* You can't wear Apple Vision Pro while wearing eyeglasses, but if you need vision correction, you can purchase ZEISS Optical Inserts, as discussed in Chapter 1.) As an example, tap Studio to brightly light up your Persona if you find it on the dim side, or tap Contour to add dramatic shadows with highlights and lowlights so it's the most flattering Persona it can be! When you finish making changes, tap Save.

If you're unable to hold Apple Vision Pro for the time it takes to capture your face, no worries! You can use Hands-Free Capture and place it on a surface at eye level, or have someone else hold it during the capture process. Just follow these steps:

1. **Open the Settings app, tap Persona, and tap Get Started.**

2. **After you refine your hands, tap the Accessibility button, and turn on Hands-Free Capture.**

3. **You can turn on Hands-Free Capture during the tutorial video or after you watch it.**

4. **Tap Save in the upper-right corner.**

5. **When instructed, take off Apple Vision Pro, set it down at eye level (or have someone else hold it), and follow the spoken instructions.**

REMEMBER

You can redo the Persona capture as often as you like if you're not happy with how you're digitally represented. To recapture your Persona:

1. **Open the Settings app and tap Persona.**

2. **Tap Edit Details or Recapture.**

3. **Use your passcode or Optic ID to authenticate yourself.**

You can't capture or edit your Persona if Travel Mode is turned on.

Step 6: Setting up Optic ID

Optic ID is similar to Face ID, which you may be familiar with on your iPhone or iPad. It's a form of biometric authentication — it uses a part of your body (your eyes) to uniquely identify you. After you've set up Optic ID, it scans your eyes to confirm you are who you say you are. This initial scan takes place immediately after setting up your Persona. It only takes a couple of seconds — just follow along with the prompts.

Just in case Optic ID can't recognize you for whatever reason, Apple Vision Pro also has you set up a passcode, which also may be required at other times, such as when installing a visionOS update.

Step 7: Activating Apple Vision Pro

After you complete all the previous steps, your Apple Vision Pro activates. Congratulations! It may take a minute or two, so be patient. Eventually, you'll see a confirmation message and hear a tone.

Next thing you know, the Home View will float in front of you with many colorful icons. This is your main home screen.

Apple Vision Pro will walk you through a quick tutorial on basic gestures and interface elements for things like selecting apps and "touching" virtual items, resizing windows to your liking, bringing up quick menus and options, and more. (Turn to Chapter 3 for more.)

Maximizing Your Experience with Apple Vision Pro

Here are some suggestions for getting the most out of your time with Apple Vision Pro:

>> **Align your eyes.** When you put on Apple Vision Pro, don't stress if the headset doesn't align with your pupils perfectly every time. Apple Vision Pro will tell you if it needs realignment, and you'll see some dotted lines around two graphics meant to represent your eyes. You'll be prompted to press and

hold the Digital Crown, so you can see a single, clear image of your content. A green check mark and high-pitch tone confirm you're good to go. If the alignment of your eyes isn't quite right when you're using Apple Vision Pro, at any time you can adjust it by opening the Settings app, tapping Eyes & Hands, and tapping Realign Displays.

» **Make sure visionOS is up to date.** As with other tech devices, updating the Apple Vision Pro operating system (known as visionOS) is important. Why? New features are added over time and various technical issues are found and addressed by Apple's engineers to enhance your experience and provide a more secure operating system. As with other Apple products, when an update is available, you'll see a little red badge in the upper-right corner of the Settings app icon on your Home View. Look at the icon and tap your fingers to open it. Then tap General and tap Software Update to download it. Make sure you have enough battery power to perform this operation (if you don't, Apple Vision Pro will warn you). You can't turn off Apple Vision Pro while it's down-loading an update.

TIP

You can still use Apple Vision Pro when the update is downloading. During the software update, Apple Vision Pro will need to restart. When it starts back up again, you'll hear a tone to confirm it's ready to use. If you've taken off the device during the software update, when you place it back on your face, you'll tap to acknowledge the operating system was updated.

» **Pay attention to Apple ID Suggestions.** When you see a badge on the Settings app, open the Settings app and tap Apple ID Suggestions. It may tell you that your Apple Vision Pro hasn't been backed up. iCloud Backup will occur automatically once a week when your Apple Vision Pro is locked and on Wi-Fi or daily when the device is also connected to power. To make changes to what's backed up, you can enter Backup Settings and prioritize certain apps, if you like.

If you see a message saying, "Your Vision Pro can't be backed up," you'll be prompted to buy additional storage in iCloud. In the United States, iCloud storage is $0.99 per month for 50 gigabytes (GB) or $2.99 for 200GB. All plans can be shared with up to five family members. Plans auto-renew every month until you cancel.

If you don't want to add more storage or back up your Apple Vision Pro at this time, but you want to get rid of the badge on the Settings app, open the Settings app, tap Apple ID Suggestions, and tap OK when it says Apple Vision Pro isn't backed up, or when it asks you to upgrade your storage, click Not Now. You'll likely continue to be reminded, however.

» **Consider your room's lighting.** Apple Vision Pro's onboard sensors and cameras require good light in order to properly map your space and accu-rately track your hand gestures. Whenever possible, try to use the device in a room with good lighting, whether that's natural light (via a nearby window) or artificial light. Apple Vision Pro will still work in a dark room, but you may need to be a little patient if some of your gestures aren't recognized at first; plus, the visual quality may not be great.

According to Apple, "As with other cameras, the cameras in Apple Vision Pro can show noise and grain when you use the device in a dim or dark environment. Turn on lamps and lights, or let in more indirect natural light during the day, to see your surroundings best."

TIP

If you like using Apple Vision Pro in the dark *a lot* — for example, if you want to use it in bed after your partner falls asleep — pick up an infrared (IR) illuminator, like the one shown in Figure 2-6, which is available for around $30. With IR light, the room will still looks dark to the human eye but will be visible by Apple Vision Pro.

TECHNICAL STUFF

An IR illuminator typically has a built-in photocell sensor that automatically turns it on in the dark (and turns it off when it's light), and through its multiple light-emitting diodes (LEDs), it emits light in the infrared range of the electromagnetic radiation spectrum.

FIGURE 2-6: The Univivi IR Illuminator is an example of an infrared illuminator, which is ideal for those who want to use Apple Vision Pro in dimly lit environments.

Courtesy of Univivi

>> **Hide other apps so you can focus.** Apple Vision Pro is a multitasker's dream — you can have multiple apps open at the same time and "pin" them to different parts of your room. This feature may be distracting, however, when you're trying to get something done, such as work on a document for your boss, or if you just want to focus exclusively on a TV show you're bingeing. To close all open apps except the one you want to keep open, simply look at the X you'd normally use to close an app, and pinch and hold on it; then tap Hide Other Apps.

Handling Apple Vision Pro

TIP

Before I wrap up this chapter, here are a few tips on properly handling Apple Vision Pro:

>> **Always pick up the device by the visor and the headband (see Figure 2-7).** Do not pick it up by the mesh Light Seal, which is just behind the visor, or you risk dropping it.

REMEMBER

The Light Seal is held on by a magnet — it can easily pop off if you pick up Apple Vision Pro by the Light Seal.

FIGURE 2-7: Remember to pick up Apple Vision Pro by the visor and the headband when taking it off and putting it back on.

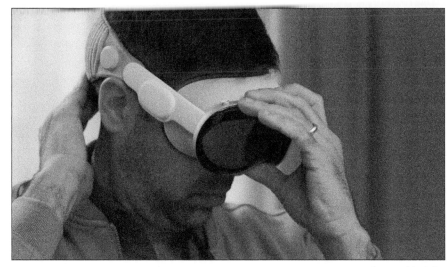

Courtesy of Apple, Inc.

» **When you aren't using Apple Vision Pro, put the soft cover on it to help prevent dust accumulation or damage.** Place Apple Vision Pro in a protective case (or at least the box it came in) to avoid accidental damage.

» **For optimal performance, keep the cover glass and displays clean and smudge free.** Only use the polishing cloth provided in the box. Do not use liquid.

» **If you need to wash the knitted parts of Apple Vision Pro, check out the instructions at** http://support.apple.com/guide/apple-vision-pro. Click Table of Contents, click Fit and Care, and click Clean Your Apple Vision Pro.

» **For optimal performance, use the included USB-C charge cable and power adapter to charge the battery.** To prevent damage to the power cable itself, avoid wrapping it too tightly around the battery when not in use.

Chapter **3**

Controlling Apple Vision Pro

A fter you've set up Apple Vision Pro, you're ready to start using it — finally! In this chapter, I discuss how best to use Apple Vision Pro. You may think the learning curve will be low — after all, the device leverages gestures in the air, your eyes, and your voice (all intuitive inputs you've already mastered in your life). But Apple Vision Pro is unique, so don't be surprised if you need a little time to fully master it.

In this chapter, I cover all the ways to control your Apple Vision Pro, including tips for getting the most out of the interface. I explain what EyeSight is and what it looks like to those around you. I also delve into the Control Center, which is an important area to know in Apple Vision Pro, as well as typing on a virtual keyboard (or physical one) for those types you may prefer an old-school interface over gestures. I also explain how to search for something in Apple Vision Pro.

Waking Up Apple Vision Pro

When you take off Apple Vision Pro, the displays turn off to save power, the device locks for security, and it goes to sleep until you need it again. If you remove the battery, however, remember to fully power down the headset first.

To power down Apple Vision Pro, press and hold the top button (over your left eye) and the Digital Crown (over your right eye), and then drag the slider. Or, open the Settings app, tap General, tap Shut Down, and then drag the slider. Or say, "Siri, turn off my Apple Vision Pro."

Assuming you didn't disconnect the battery or shut down Apple Vision Pro manually, you can quickly wake and unlock Apple Vision Pro when you want to use it again. Just put it back on! Placing Apple Vision Pro over your head and face triggers the headset to detect your eyes (via Optic ID), and the displays turn on for you. Just look at the Optic ID icon until Apple Vision Pro unlocks.

You'll be notified if you need to reposition the Apple Vision Pro slightly. You may need to adjust the headset a little and tighten the Solo Knit Band with the dial on the right side of your head (turn clockwise to tighten, counterclockwise to loosen).

If you didn't create a passcode or enable Optic ID during setup, you'll be prompted to do so now.

REMEMBER

Depending on what you're doing with Apple Vision Pro, you must use a passcode instead of Optic ID. For example, a passcode is required when you restart Apple Vision Pro or if it has been more than 48 hours since you last unlocked Apple Vision Pro.

TIP

If you don't like where the list of Apple Vision Pro apps are seen in your room, maybe because they're somewhat obstructed by a piece of furniture, simply look to an open space where you are and press and hold the Digital Crown (above your right eye) to move the list of apps to where you're looking.

Navigating Apple Vision Pro

The three main ways you interface with Apple Vision Pro are with your eyes, gestures, and voice. There are a couple of button presses here and there, too, like the Digital Crown on the top right of the headset and the top button on the top left of the headset.

In the following sections, I walk you through all these options for navigating.

Using hand gestures and eye movements

You'll mostly control your Apple Vision Pro with your eyes (in other words, where you look inside the headset) coupled with hand movements in the air.

Here are the most common hand and eye gestures, what they do, and how to do them.

» **Tapping your fingers together:** The easiest way to do this is to tap your index finger with your thumb on your left or right hand (but it works with other fingers, too). This gesture opens apps and select options, kind of like clicking something with a mouse, tapping on a phone or tablet screen, or pressing the Enter button.

» **Touching an item:** Whether it's picking up an object in a game (like a sword) typing on a virtual keyboard floating in front of you, or playing a digital piano in a music lesson, you can interact with certain elements directly with your outstretched fingers. Pretend that object you see is really there and touch it.

» **Pinching and holding:** When you're using Apple Vision Pro, you may want to see additional options for a task. Or you may want to zoom in and out of something. You can do both of these things by pinching and holding your thumb and index finger together. This is kind of like right-clicking on a computer mouse, which brings up options to select.

Here are some other times you can pinch and hold:

- Look at the small circle at the bottom of every app and it will turn into an X to close the app (see Figure 3-1). Tap to confirm this is what you want to do. Or, pinch and hold over the X button at the bottom of an app to see additional options, such as Close All Other Open Apps.

- Depending on the app, you can pinch and hold with both hands at the same time and pull your hands apart to zoom in or move them closer to zoom out, like resizing a window.

FIGURE 3-1:
The X at the
bottom of the
app allows you
to close it.

» **Pinching and dragging:** Pinch and hold to grab something you see in Apple Vision Pro — like a photo, a window bar, or other content — and then drag it wherever you like.

At the bottom of every app, next to the circle icon, which turns to an X (to close the app), there is a horizontal "window bar" (see Figure 3-2). You can look at this bar and move the window around your view (of the real environment you're in) and let go to pin it there. You can open another app and pin it somewhere else, too. Why would you want to do this? Maybe you want to watch a baseball game *and* work on a document or browse the web at the same time (or do all three). Check out Figure 3-3 for an illustration of what that will look like.

Alternatively, you can pinch and drag a shape in a Freeform board (see Chapter 16). Pinch and drag to scroll up and down or side to side. When looking at images in the Photos app, for example, you can scroll through your various albums. Swipe to scroll and tap to stop scrolling (see Chapter 13).

» **Swiping:** You can scroll through content quickly by pinching and quickly flicking your wrist, left and right or up and down.

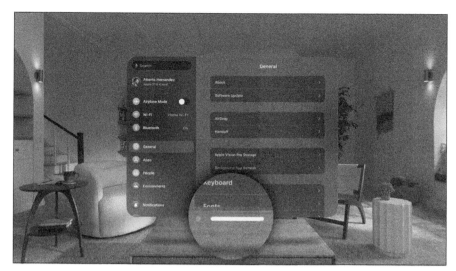

Courtesy of Apple, Inc.

Courtesy of Apple, Inc.

Using your voice

Most Apple Vision Pro owners use their hands and eyes to interact with content, but you can also use your voice. In fact, using your voice may be the preferred way to use Apple Vision Pro, especially if you have dexterity challenges. (I cover accessibility features later in this chapter.)

You can speak commands to perform gestures, interact with interface elements, dictate and edit text, and more.

Setting up Voice Control

Setting up Voice Control on Apple Vision Pro is simple. It just requires a one-time download. Your headset will need to be connected to Wi-Fi in order to get this download, but you won't need an internet connection after that to use Voice Control.

To get started, follow these steps:

1. **Open the Settings app, tap Accessibility, and tap Voice Control.**

2. **Tap Set Up Voice Control, and then tap Continue to start the file download to your device.**

   When the download is complete, the Voice Control icon (which looks like a microphone) appears in the status bar to indicate Voice Control is turned on.

Now you've got a few things to set up before you can begin:

>> **Language:** Set your desired language and/or download languages for offline use.

>> **Vocabulary:** Teach Voice Control new words.

>> **Show Confirmation:** When Voice Control recognizes a command, a visual confirmation appears at the top of your view. This option is turned on by default.

>> **Play Sound:** When Voice Control recognizes a command, an audible sound is played. This option is turned on by default.

>> **Show Hints:** See command suggestions and hints.

>> **Overlay:** Display numbers, names, or a grid over interface elements.

Turning Voice Control on or off

After you set up Voice Control, you can turn it on or off, as you see fit, in one of two ways:

>> Activate Siri and say, "Turn on Voice Control" or "Turn off Voice Control."

>> Add Voice Control to Accessibility Shortcuts, to turn Voice Control on or off.

Finding out about Voice Control commands

After you've enabled Voice Control, you can use the following commands:

>> "Open Control Center."

>> "Go home."

>> "Tap [item name]."

>> "Open [app name]."

>> "Take screenshot."

>> "Turn up volume."

Need some help? You can always say "Show me what to say" or "Show commands" to learn more about Voice Control commands. Or open the Settings app, tap Accessibility, tap Voice Control, and tap Open Voice Control Guide.

Considering a screen overlay

For faster interactions, you can opt to have Apple Vision Pro show you a screen overlay for item names, numbers, or a grid:

>> **Item names:** Say, "Show names" or "Show names continuously." Then say, "Tap [item name]."

>> **Numbers:** Say, "Show numbers" or "Show numbers continuously." Then say the number next to the item you want.

>> **Grid:** To interact with a screen location not represented by an item name or number, you can say, "Show grid" or "Show grid continuously." Then say a number to show a more detailed grid or say a command to interact with an area of the grid.

To turn off the visual overlay, say "Hide names," "Hide numbers," or "Hide grid."

Switching between modes

You can switch between Dictation mode, Spelling mode, and Command mode. For example, if you're working on an email or a document, you can easily switch between verbal inputs, based on your preferences.

By default, *Dictation mode* means any words you say (that aren't Voice Control commands) are entered as text, as you say them.

When you're in Dictation mode and you need to spell out a word, simply say "Spelling mode," which spells out words based on the letters you say verbally. To switch back to Dictation mode, say "Dictation mode."

In *Command mode,* those words are not inputted as text. Use this when you want Voice Control to respond only to commands (and not have Apple Vision Pro enter what you're saying as text). To switch to Command mode, say "Command mode." To switch back to Dictation mode, say "Dictation mode."

Using Siri

You can also summon Siri, your hands-free personal assistant, to help you do more with Apple Vision Pro. Just as you may wake up your digital companion on virtually all other Apple products — iPhone, iPad, Mac, Apple Watch, HomePod, and Apple TV — you can summon Siri to do all sorts of things with Apple Vision Pro.

For example, ask Siri to open apps and interact with content, set an alarm, get a weather report, send a message, pull up information about a person, place or thing, and much more.

Just like on other devices, some Siri requests can be handled on Apple Vision Pro itself, like setting a reminder about something. Other tasks require the internet, like asking how tall Tom Hanks is (6 feet, if you were curious).

The first step, though, is to set up Siri. If you didn't set up Siri when you first booted up Apple Vision Pro, open the Settings app, tap Siri & Search, tap Listen For, and tap whichever option you prefer. You can also activate Siri by typing (see the accessibility section later in this chapter).

Just like on your other Apple devices, you can change Siri's voice by opening the Settings app, tapping Siri & Search, tapping Siri Voice, and tapping the option you prefer.

To activate (waken) Siri, say, "Hey, Siri" or "Siri," and then ask a question or make a request, such as "Siri, what time is it in Paris?" or look at an app and say "Hey, Siri. Open this."

You'll see that familiar semitransparent circle appear in the lower part of the screen to confirm Siri is "thinking" of its response to you. Unlike on iPhone, iPad, and Mac, however, this icon is in 3D (see Figure 3-4).

TIP

What if your dog's name is "Sari" and Apple Vision Pro keeps thinking you're saying "Siri"? To prevent the headset from responding to "Siri," open the Settings app, tap Siri & Search, tap Listen For, and tap Off.

FIGURE 3-4:
This icon means Siri is "thinking" of a response.

If Siri misunderstands you, try being more specific or saying your request in a different way. For example, if Siri doesn't understand "What was the biggest song in 1970?" try something like "What was the biggest pop song in the United States in 1970?"

You can also spell out part of your request, if that helps, such as saying "Call A-L-E-X."

If you want to cancel your Siri request, say "Cancel" or press the Digital Crown to close Siri.

On a related note, if you're using Siri to send messages, you can change a message to someone before sending it, by saying "Change it" or cancel it altogether by saying "Cancel."

Especially because you don't have a physical keyboard and mouse, or a screen to tap, Siri works great with Apple Vision Pro. Not sure where to start? Ask Siri what it can do for you by simply asking Siri what it can do! If you need some inspiration, here are some requests to try:

>> "Siri, call my brother."

>> "Siri, send a message to Mom."

- "Siri, read my [emails or messages]."

- "Siri, open the Notes app."

- "Siri, what Environments do I have?" (See Chapter 4 for more on Environments.)

- "Siri, add tomatoes to the grocery list."

- "Siri, show me my Persona." (See Chapter 2 for more on Personas.)

- "Siri, turn off my Apple Vision Pro."

- "Siri, set up a meeting with Katherine on Wednesday at 10 a.m." (This creates an event in Calendar.)

- "Siri, what's my update?" (This gives you a personalized update about local weather, news, calendar events, reminders, and more.)

TIP

For more on Siri, check out *Siri For Dummies* by yours truly (published by Wiley).

Using the Digital Crown and top button

The Digital Crown is both a raised circular button and a dial on the top right of the headset (above your right eye). The top button is a flatter, oval-shaped button on the top left of the headset (above your left eye). Both can be used in multiple scenarios:

- **Opening Home View:** When you open Home View, which is like the Home Screen on your iPhone or iPad, you'll see your circular icons clumped together, each representing a different app (see Figure 3-5).

  To open Home View in any app you're in, press the Digital Crown or open Control Center and then tap the Home View button.

  Home View also includes quick access to People and Environments (see Chapter 4), but the default view is of your apps.

- **Recentering your content in your view:** Press and hold the Digital Crown to recenter what you're looking at. Why would you want to do this? Maybe something in the (real) room you're in is blocking the content you're trying to see in Apple Vision Pro. Look to an open space and press the Digital Crown, and the content will pop up there.

- **Adjusting immersion or volume:** Just like on Apple Watch, the Digital Crown in a ridged button you can turn like a dial. For example, in Home View, you can choose to have Environments (like wallpaper) that stretch all around if you, if you like. When you're in Environments, look up to the Volume icon at the top of your view while turning the Digital Crown to make it louder or softer (see Chapter 4 for more on Environments).

FIGURE 3-5:
My Home
View screen.

Courtesy of Marc Saltzman

You can also open Control Center, drag the volume slider left or right, or use Siri to say something like, "Siri, set volume to 100 percent" or "Siri, lower the volume."

>> **Switching between your surroundings and digital content:** If you double-click the Digital Crown, it will switch to a view of your surroundings in real life. To return to your Apple Vision Pro experience, press the Digital Crown once.

>> **Opening Capture:** Ready to snap a pic or shoot videos using your headset? Press the top button, which is over your left eye. Chapter 13 discusses how to capture, view, and share spatial photos and videos via Apple Vision Pro.

>> **Capturing a still image of your view:** To capture a photo of what you see inside of Apple Vision Pro (like a screenshot), simultaneously press and release the top button and Digital Crown. Or say "Siri, take a screenshot."

>> **Using an accessibility shortcut:** Later in this chapter, I share several accessibility features built into Apple Vision Pro, but to open these options, simply triple-click the Digital Crown.

>> **Force-quitting an app:** If you want to get out of an app — and close it as opposed to just minimizing it — simultaneously press and hold the top button and Digital Crown until you see the words Force Quit Applications. Then tap the name of the app you want to close and tap Force Quit.

>> **Turning on Apple Vision Pro:** If your headset is in standby mode, you can just put on Apple Vision Pro and it will boot up. But if you powered it down or the battery wasn't charged up, press and hold the top button until the Apple logo appears on the front display and the power cable light comes on.

- >> **Turning off Apple Vision Pro:** Simultaneously press and hold the top button and Digital Crown until the sliders appear (Force Quit Applications will appear first); then drag the top slider to power off. Or open the Settings app, tap General, and tap Shut Down.

- >> **Force-restarting:** You shouldn't need to do this very often, but to force-restart your Apple Vision Pro, simultaneously press and hold the top button and Digital Crown until Apple Vision Pro powers off (Force Quit Applications and the power slider will appear first).

TIP

If you're wearing Apple Vision Pro and you want to see the room you're actually in — unobstructed by apps, icons, images, and such — you don't need to take the headset off. Instead, press the Digital Crown on the upper right of the Apple Vision Pro to clear your (digital) view of content so you can see or do something in real life, like use a laptop, feed your fish, or make a sandwich! When you're ready to see stuff inside Apple Vision Pro again, press the Digital Crown one more time.

Understanding EyeSight on Apple Vision Pro

As the name of this feature suggests, EyeSight reveals your eyes on the front of your Apple Vision Pro headset, designed to let those nearby know whether you're available to chat or fully immersed in an experience.

EyeSight is not a real-time look at your eyes (like a see-through visor). Instead, your personalized EyeSight is based on a previously captured image of your eyes.

When you're wearing Apple Vision Pro and you've captured your Persona upon setup (see Chapter 2), EyeSight is personalized with your own eyes. Your Persona is used primarily for FaceTime calls, but it's also an option while collaborating in some apps and games. If you haven't yet captured your Persona, EyeSight shows an impression (a generic image) of "your" eyes — without any personal details.

EyeSight only appears when you're wearing the device and others are around you. The front visor shows the Apple logo when you turn on Apple Vision Pro and a progress bar when you update visionOS.

As shown in Figure 3-6, there are three views of EyeSight, which tells people around you what you're currently experiencing with Apple Vision Pro:

FIGURE 3-6:
The three
views of Apple's
EyeSight feature
on Apple
Vision Pro.

Courtesy of Apple, Inc.

>> On the left, the person's EyeSight is visible, which lets others know that the person wearing Apple Vision Pro can see them.

>> In the middle, the person's EyeSight is dimmed, to let others know the person wearing Apple Vision Pro is working in apps and may not be able to see them.

>> On the right, the person's EyeSight is completely hidden to let others know that they're fully immersed. That is, if the person is in an interactive experience, EyeSight shows an animation to let others know you may not be able to see them.

When you're capturing spatial photos and videos (see Chapter 13), capturing your view, or sharing your view with others, EyeSight shows an animation letting people know that you're using the camera.

Although Apple Vision Pro uses your own eyes to personalize your EyeSight — after you've captured your Persona — Apple lets you delete your personalized EyeSight if you want. If you delete your personalized EyeSight, it will revert back to the *impression* of your eyes that others will see.

TIP

Deleting your personalized EyeSight does not impact your Persona.

To delete your personalized EyeSight, open the Settings app, tap People Awareness, and tap Delete EyeSight.

If you delete your personalized EyeSight and want to use it again later, you'll need to recapture your Persona.

Understanding Apple Vision Pro's Control Center

Control Center gives you quick access to useful controls and features. It lets you easily search, adjust the volume, check battery level, see the current date and time, and set up things like screen sharing, guest users, travel mode, and more.

Opening Control Center

Look up with your eyes while wearing Apple Vision Pro (no need to move your head), and you'll see a little icon appear with an arrow pointing down (see Figure 3-7). This is the Control Center button.

Control Center button

FIGURE 3-7: The Control Center button appears when you look up.

TIP

If you don't see the Control Center button, exit out of the app you're in, so you see the Home View (see Chapter 4) and then look up again. Still don't see it? Make sure there are no apps toward the top of your view.

TIP

The Control Center button may be different colors, depending on what you're doing in Apple Vision Pro at that time.

Some people have trouble seeing the Control Center. In my experience, it's because they're tilting their head to look up rather than looking up with their eyes only. It takes some practice, but you'll get it.

TIP

You can change how high up you need to look to see the Control Center button. Just open the Settings app, tap Control Center, and then choose how high or low you want the button to appear.

Setting Control Center access

When you open Control Center, you'll see the following (see Figure 3-8):

>> **The current time.**

>> **Today's day and date.**

>> **Wi-Fi signal strength or the Personal Hotspot icon if your Apple Vision Pro is connected to one.**

>> **Focus icon (like Do Not Disturb) if active.**

>> **Battery status or the green battery charging icon.**

>> **Green dot:** This means camera is in use. The dot appears if an app or feature is using your Apple Vision Pro's camera at this moment.

>> **Orange dot:** This means the microphone is in use. The dot appears when an app or feature is using the device's microphone at that time.

>> **Blue dot:** This means your location information is known. The dot appears when an app or service is accessing your location.

>> **Home View icon:** Takes you to the Home View (see Chapter 4).

>> **Environments:** This lets you change your virtual background (see Chapter 4).

>> **Notification Center:** A list of your apps and what notifications you've allowed for each.

>> **Siri:** You'll see the Siri icon (if you enabled Type to Siri).

>> **Volume slider:** Shows the level of volume.

>> **More Control Center options:** Tapping this icon (the second from the right) takes you to the second Control Center screen, which has the following:

- **Wi-Fi:** Colored blue if it's connected. Tap to change Wi-Fi networks.

- **Airplane Mode:** Toggle on or off. Turing it on turns off all wireless radios, like Wi-Fi and Bluetooth.

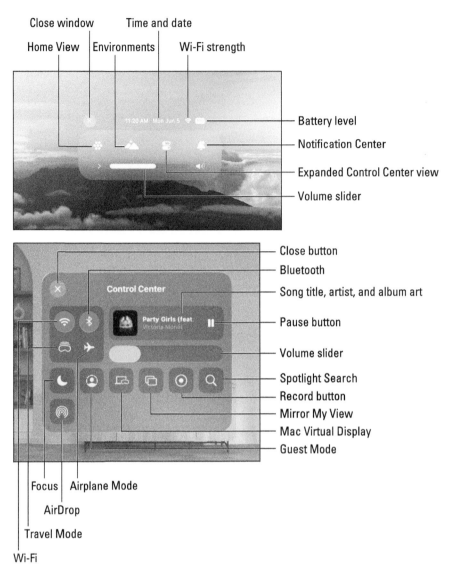

Close window

Home View Environments Time and date

Wi-Fi strength

Battery level

Notification Center

Expanded Control Center view

Volume slider

Close button

Bluetooth

Control Center

Song title, artist, and album art

Party Girls (feat.
Victoria Monét

Pause button

Volume slider

Spotlight Search

Record button

Mirror My View

Mac Virtual Display

Guest Mode

FIGURE 3-8:
The top image
shows the
main Control
Center view.
The bottom
image shows
an expanded
set of options
in Control
Center.

Focus Airplane Mode

AirDrop

Travel Mode

Wi-Fi

Courtesy of Apple, Inc.

- **Travel Mode** (see later in this chapter).

- **Bluetooth:** Colored blue if it's connected. Tap to change paired devices.

- **Song, podcast, or video that's playing.**

- **Focus,** such as Do Not Disturb, Work, Personal (see Chapter 16).

- **Guest Mode:** When you share your Apple Vision Pro with another person (see later this chapter).

- **Mac Virtual Display:** Use your Apple Vision Pro as your Mac's monitor (see Chapter 16).

- **Mirror My View:** Wirelessly share what your Apple Vision Pro looks like to a nearby external display such as iPhone, iPad, Mac, Apple TV, or some Smart TVs (see Chapter 16).

- **Record button:** Screen recording (see Chapter 13).

- **Spotlight Search:** Use this to find something on your Apple Vision Pro (it launches the keyboard).

- **AirDrop:** To wirelessly send files, such as photos, to a nearby compatible device.

Changing Control Center options

You can add or remove Control Center options, if you like. For example, if you never use a particular feature, you can drop it from the Control Center so it isn't in your way.

Just open the Settings app, tap Control Center, and then add or remove the controls as you see fit. To add, tap the green plus button next to the control you want to add. To remove, tap the option and then tap the red minus button.

Typing on a Virtual Keyboard in Apple Vision Pro

Much of what you do in Apple Vision Pro involves eye movements, in-air gestures, and your voice, but a virtual (digital) keyboard pops up when you need to type something. (Later in this chapter, I explain how you can also add a physical keyboard and mouse, if you like.)

When you tap a text field in an app — for example, if you just started a new note, document, or email — the virtual keyboard built into Apple Vision Pro automatically appears on the bottom half of your view (see Figure 3-9). Stretch out your hands as if you're about to type on a real keyboard, and you'll see this floating one works great.

Courtesy of Apple, Inc.

You have options on how you "type":

>> Look at each key, and then tap together two fingers (such as your index finger and your thumb).

>> Touch keys on the virtual keyboard (using up to one finger on each hand). This is the hunt-and-peck method.

>> To show special characters and accents, pinch and hold or directly touch and hold a letter.

The text you're entering will appear in the preview at the top of the keyboard.

TIP

If you don't clearly see the virtual keyboard in front of you, simply recenter your view by pressing and holding the Digital Crown. Or walk forward toward the float-ing keyboard, if possible. Or grab the horizontal window bar at the bottom of the keyboard, drag it around, and let go where you want it. The keyboard is semi-transparent, so you can still see the app or other content behind it.

To close the keyboard, look below it at the small circle, and it will change into an X. Tap the X to close the keyboard.

When you're asking to type in a passcode or PIN, you'll see what looks like a numeric keypad. Simply press the numbers as you would with a real number pad.

TIP

A few other considerations when "typing" on Apple Vision Pro:

>> **Selecting text:** Double-tap a word in the text field and then pinch and drag either end of the selected text to add or remove text in the selection.

>> **Deleting text:** To remove a few characters, tap or touch the Delete key. Or pinch and hold, or touch and hold, to quickly delete several characters at a time.

>> **Deleting large amounts of text:** Select all the text you want to delete; then tap or touch the Delete key.

>> **Changing typing assistance options:** You can change many keyboard options, such as enabling or disabling auto-correction or turning on smart punctuation (for example, having two hyphens automatically change to a dash), and so on. These settings apply to your virtual keyboard and an optional external keyboard. Open the Settings app, tap General, and then tap Keyboard. In the All Keyboards list, turn typing features on or off.

Searching on Apple Vision Pro

If you're trying to find something on your Apple Vision Pro — an app, content with an app, an image, a setting, or a feature — you can use the included search to find almost anything.

There are two ways to search effectively:

>> Open Control Center, tap the Options button, and then tap the Search button. Enter what you're looking for in the Search field, and then tap a result. You can also look at the Dictation button (microphone icon) in the Search field, or tap or touch the Dictation button in the virtual keyboard and then say what you're looking for.

>> Summon Siri. Simply say "Siri, [your request]" such as "Siri, open Display settings," and it'll work.

Adding a Keyboard, Trackpad, or Game Controller to Apple Vision Pro

You can add a wireless keyboard and/or trackpad to Apple Vision Pro if you prefer navigating that way. Because you can see through your Apple Vision Pro headset, you can place the keyboard and/or trackpad on a desk or table just as you would if you weren't wearing a headset.

Apple Magic Keyboard and Apple Magic Trackpad both work with Apple Vision Pro, as do most other Bluetooth devices. But be aware that Apple Vision Pro is *not* compatible with older models of Apple keyboards and trackpads that use removable batteries, and Apple Vision Pro does not work with Bluetooth mice.

TIP

If you have any doubt about compatibility, head to www.apple.com/shop/vision/accessories — anything listed there is compatible. You can also call Apple at 800–692–7753 or go to the nearest Apple Store.

After you've found a compatible device, the first step is to enter pairing mode on the device you want to connect. Then, in Apple Vision Pro, open the Settings app, tap Bluetooth, and tap the device's name. Then you should be good to go.

If you're experiencing any performance issues, open the Settings app, tap Accessibility, tap Keyboards, and tap Full Keyboard Access, to ensure it's enabled.

Note: When you're using a Bluetooth keyboard, in some cases a minimized version of a virtual keyboard will appear on the screen so you can still use gestures to select and edit text, if you want. Tap the Show Keyboard button in the corner, if it doesn't appear.

If you're into gaming, you can add a controller to Apple Vision Pro and play games with it, as long as the game itself supports a wireless controller. All controllers with MFi (Made for iPhone) designation work with Apple Vision Pro, which includes controllers by Xbox, PlayStation, and any controller that works with iPadOS. Figure 3-10 shows an example of this in action.

FIGURE 3-10:
Want to kick back and play a basketball video game? Bluetooth controllers will work with select games.

Courtesy of Take-Two Interactive Software, Inc.

Identifying the Accessibility Features of Apple Vision Pro

Apple Vision Pro is packed with a variety of accessibility features. In fact, you can turn on many accessibility features right when you first set up Apple Vision Pro. If you want to turn on accessibility features after your initial setup, you can choose one of the following options:

» Triple-click the top button (over your left eye) to access accessibility settings.

» Open the Settings app and tap Accessibility.

Here's a complete list of the accessibility options:

» **Vision**

- **VoiceOver:** VoiceOver is a gesture-based screen reader that gives audible descriptions of what's on your screen. To turn it on, triple-click the Digital Crown.

- **Zoom:** Zoom magnifies content, including text. To turn it on, in the Settings app, tap Accessibility and tap Zoom.

- **Display & Text Size:** You can enlarge the font, add bold text, increase contrast, and more. To adjust these options, in the Settings app, tap Accessibility and tap Display & Text Size.

- **Motion:** If you have sensitivity to motion effects or movement in your view, you can adjust the motion settings. In the Settings app, tap Accessibility and then tap Motion.

- **Spoken Content:** Similar to VoiceOver, you can hear Apple Vision Pro speak the text in your view and provide typing feedback. To turn it on, in the Settings app, tap Accessibility and then tap Spoken Content.

- **Audio Descriptions:** If you have video content that includes audio descriptions of scenes, Apple Vision Pro can play the descriptions for you. To turn it on, in the Settings app, tap Accessibility and then tap Audio Descriptions.

- **Eye Input:** If you aren't able to navigate with two eyes, you can just use one eye. In the Settings app, tap Accessibility and then tap Eye Input.

» **Physical and motor**

- **AssistiveTouch:** This feature helps you use Apple Vision Pro, even if you have difficulty interacting with visionOS or pressing buttons. In the Settings app, tap Accessibility, tap Interaction, and tap AssistiveTouch.

- **Sound Actions:** You can assign a sound to perform actions, such as tapping or adjusting volume. In the Settings app, tap Accessibility, tap Interaction, tap Sound Actions, tap a sound, and then assign an action to it.

- **Dwell Control:** Dwell Control makes it easier to perform actions exclusively with your eyes by allowing you to interact with controls when you keep your eyes fixed on them for a selected amount of time. In the Settings app, tap Accessibility, tap Interaction, tap AssistiveTouch, and turn on Dwell Control.

- **Switch Control:** If you have physical challenges, use Switch Control to operate Apple Vision Pro using one or more switches (via Bluetooth). In the Settings app, tap Accessibility, tap Switch Control, and tap Switches.

- **Pointer Control:** You can use your eyes, head, wrist, or finger as a pointer with Apple Vision Pro. You can also adjust the appearance of the pointer by tweaking its color, shape, size, scrolling speed, and more. In the Settings app, tap Accessibility, tap Interaction, and tap Pointer Control.

- **Voice Control:** You can control Apple Vision Pro with just your voice — for example, by speaking commands to perform gestures, interact with elements, dictate and edit text, and more. In the Settings app, tap Accessibility and tap Voice Control.

- **Digital Crown:** You can adjust the speed of button presses for the Digital Crown. In the Settings app, tap Accessibility and tap Digital Crown.

- **Keyboards:** You can adjust the virtual keyboard, such as setting the virtual keyboard to only display uppercase letters. In the Settings app, tap Accessibility and tap Keyboards.

- **AirPods:** If you own a pair of third-generation AirPods (or newer), AirPods Pro (all generations), or AirPods Max, you can adjust the accessibility settings to suit your motor or hearing needs. In the Settings app, tap Accessibility and tap AirPods.

» Hearing

- **Hearing Devices:** You can pair any Made for iPhone (MFi) hearing aids or sound processors with Apple Vision Pro and adjust their settings. In the Settings app, tap Accessibility and tap Hearing Devices.

- **Audio/Visual:** You can adjust mono audio or left–right stereo balance to suit your specific hearing needs. In the Settings app, tap Accessibility and then tap Audio/Visual.

- **Sound Recognition:** Apple Vision Pro can continuously listen for certain sounds (like a doorbell or a crying baby) and notify you when it recognizes these sounds. This feature isn't perfect, so don't rely on it exclusively, but it may be a handy option. In the Settings app, tap Accessibility and tap Sound Recognition.

- **Background Sounds:** You can play calming sounds in the background (rain, crashing waves, and so on) while using Apple Vision Pro, perhaps to mask environmental noise. In the Settings app, tap Accessibility, tap Audio/Visual, and tap Background Sounds.

- **Subtitles and Captioning:** In supported apps, Apple Vision Pro can display subtitles, closed captions, and transcriptions, allowing people with hearing impairment to follow along more easily with audio and video. In the Settings app, tap Accessibility and tap Subtitles & Captioning.

» General

- **Guided Access:** Guided Access helps you stay focused on a task by temporarily restricting Apple Vision Pro to a single app. In the Settings app, tap Accessibility and tap Guided Access.

- **Siri:** You can use your voice to summon Siri, which can help you turn many accessibility features on or off, make and receive FaceTime calls, send messages, look up information, and so much more. In the Settings app, tap Accessibility and tap Siri.

- **Accessibility Shortcut:** For the accessibility setting you use the most, you can create an easy-to-access shortcut on Apple Vision Pro, to quickly turn it on or off. For example, use Siri to say something like "Turn on VoiceOver" or triple-click the Digital Crown to quickly turn on or off accessibility features by triple-clicking the Digital Crown. In the Settings app, tap Accessibility and tap Accessibility Shortcut.

- **Per-App Settings:** You can customize accessibility settings for specific apps on Apple Vision Pro, as well as Home View (see Chapter 4), Settings, and more. In the Settings app, tap Accessibility and tap Per-App Settings.

Enabling Travel Mode on Apple Vision Pro

If your Apple Vision Pro headset senses that you're on an airplane, it may ask if you want to turn on Travel Mode, which adapts to the motion for a better viewing (and smoother controlling) experience. The headset relies on an array of sensors that see the environment around you and can make some adjustments to keep your view stable.

If Apple Vision Pro doesn't detect that you're on a plane, you can turn on Travel Mode any time in Control Center (a good idea to do so before boarding):

1. **Look up inside Apple Vision Pro until you see the Control Center button, and tap the button to open Control Center.**

2. **Tap the Options button.**

3. **Tap the Travel Mode button.**

   It looks like a shaky headset.

4. **Tap Turn On Travel Mode to confirm.**

To exit Travel Mode, go back to Control Center, tap the Options button, and tap Turn Off.

TIP

Though it doesn't happen often, Apple Vision Pro may think you're on an airplane when you're not. If this happen, you should choose *not* to activate Travel Mode if prompted to.

Want to watch a TV show or movie while reclining in an airplane seat? Figure 3-11 shows what it could look like.

FIGURE 3-11:
If you don't care what you look like wearing your Apple Vision Pro on a plane, kick back and watch content on the equivalent of a 100+-inch screen! And make sure to use AirPods (or other wireless earbuds) for private listening!

Courtesy of Apple, Inc.

TIP

When using Travel Mode, take heed of the following suggestions from Apple, which I've paraphrased for you here:

>> In Travel mode, remember to stay seated while using Apple Vision Pro. If you're going to stand up, first take off your Apple Vision Pro.

>> On an airplane, remove your Apple Vision Pro during taxiing, takeoff, and landing (you'll likely be instructed to do so anyway). Also remove it if the flight has turbulence, so you can focus on staying safe.

>> If you can, avoid looking out the airplane window, because doing so can affect your headset's ability to properly track your surroundings. Closing the blinds will give you the best experience anyway.

>> If the content you're viewing in Apple Vision Pro looks a little tilted or off-center, press the Digital Crown button (over your right eye) to recenter your view.

>> Restarting Apple Vision Pro will turn off Travel Mode.

If you have Pointer Control turned on (in the Settings app, tap Accessibility, tap Interaction, tap Pointer Control), and your head is set as the pointer, Apple says you may not be able to turn on Travel Mode after the airplane begins moving. Instead, turn on Travel Mode before you board the plane or when you find your seat. (Then remove Apple Vision Pro for takeoff and put it back on when it's safe to do so.)

Also note that Persona isn't available when you're using Travel Mode. See Chapter 2 for more on Persona.

Finally, if you flew somewhere to buy Apple Vision Pro and you're eager to use it before you get home, know that you can't set up your new headset while traveling on an airplane. You'll need to do it while not moving at more than 500 miles per hour!

Setting Up a Guest Session on Your Apple Vision Pro

If your family and friends are like mine, they've walked in and seen you wearing Apple Vision Pro and asked if they can try it on and experience it for themselves. This is even better than sharing your Apple Vision Pro view to another screen in your room, because they can really get a sense of the spatial computing magic by donning the headset.

You can take off Apple Vision Pro and hand it to someone else to try, but because your eyes and hands were scanned specifically for you, the experience may not be as good for them as it is for you.

For this reason, Apple lets you set up a Guest User so you can share your Apple Vision Pro with someone else and give them the quality experience you've come to expect. Plus, you get to choose what the Guest User can open and what they can't (see Figure 3-12).

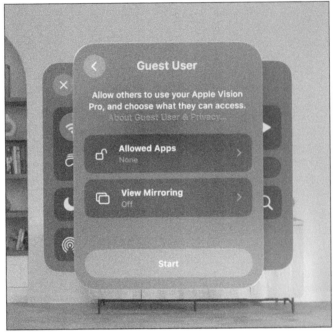

FIGURE 3-12: By setting up a Guest User in Apple Vision Pro, you can choose what your family and friends can open — and what they can't.

Guests complete eye and hand setup when they put on Apple Vision Pro, but the eye and hand settings will revert to yours when the Guest User session ends.

Guest users can't access your Optic ID (using your unique irises to identify you), Apple Pay (to buy something), EyeSight (how your eyes look to others through the visor), and Persona (a virtual representation of yourself).

Setting up a Guest User session is easy. Just follow these steps:

1. **Open Control Center by looking up while wearing the headset and tapping the Control Center button.**

2. **Tap the Options button.**

3. **Tap the Guest User button.**

It looks like a person inside a dotted circle.

4. **Tweak the settings as you see fit.**

Your options include the following:

WARNING

REMEMBER

- **Allowed Apps:** Select whether a guest user can access only open apps or all apps. Tap the small arrow and allow or disallow certain apps.

If you grant a guest full access to all apps, they'll have access to your information in those apps, such as your Safari browsing history, Messages, Mail, and Calendar. Some options may require that you set a passcode, which you'll need to share with the guest, but remember to change it immediately afterward. (Changing passcodes is covered in Chapter 5, which is all about customizing Settings.)

Guests cannot access your Optic ID, Apple Pay, EyeSight, or Persona.

- **View Mirroring:** If you want to see what a guest is doing while using your Apple Vision Pro, tap View Mirroring. Then choose a compatible device from the list of available devices.

To start a Guest User session, follow these steps:

1. **Open Control Center by looking up while wearing the headset and tapping the Control Center button.**

2. **Tap the Options button.**

3. **Tap the Guest User button.**

4. **Tap Start.**

5. **Remove Apple Vision Pro from your head and let the guest put it on.**

If Apple Vision Pro is not put on within 5 minutes, the session automatically ends. (If you have a passcode, the device also automatically locks.)

When your guest is finished using your Apple Vision Pro, they can take it off to end the session. (Or they can open Control Center, tap the Control Center button, tap the Options button, tap Guest User, and tap End Session. But why do all that when they can just take it off?)

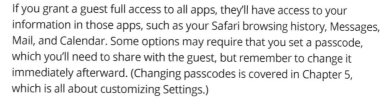

REMEMBER

Just like when you put on Apple Vision Pro for the first time, your guest may need to adjust the fit so it's comfortable (see Chapter 2), or they may need a different size Light Seal or headband for a snug and comfortable fit.

IN THIS CHAPTER

» Navigating Apple Vision Pro's
Home View

» Using and downloading apps from
the App Store

» Contacting friends, family, and
colleagues

» Choosing and changing an
Environment

Chapter **4**

Using the Home View

T his chapter covers what the main Home View is all about. It introduces you to the apps that come with Apple Vision Pro and walks you through how to download more apps from the App Store. I also show you how to use the People tab to contact friends and family. And I explain how to choose and change an Environment. And Home View is the launching pad for it all.

Getting to Know Home View

Home View is like your Mac's desktop or your iPhone or iPad's Home Screen. Home View lets you see and access three things:

» **Apps:** Represented by a large *A*, these are your applications. They may be spread out across multiple pages, just like on an iPhone or iPad.

» **People:** Represented by an icon that looks like two people, this gives you quick access to people you mostly chat with. It's a shortcut to connect to others.

» **Environments:** Resembling two mountains, and covered later in this chapter, Environments is kind of like wallpaper, but cooler.

By default, your apps will take up most of the screen, as shown in Figure 4-1. To the left of this view, you'll see the tab bar, which enables you to switch between Apps, People, and Environments.

Courtesy of Apple, Inc.

FIGURE 4-1:
A close-up view
of Apple Vision
Pro's main
Home View,
with a handful
of apps front
and center.

You can get to Home View quickly, no matter what app you're in on Apple Vision Pro. To open Home View, do either of the following:

>> **Press the Digital Crown.** This is the button above your right eye.

>> **Open Control Center and tap the Home View button, which looks like a circle comprised of seven big dots.** For more on how to access Control Center, turn to Chapter 5.

Accessing Apps on Apple Vision Pro

Apple Vision Pro comes preloaded with dozens of great apps to get you started.

In Home View, you can swipe left or right to see them all — just pinch your index finger and thumb together and drag them to the left or right, as if you were turning a page or pulling a thread.

To launch an app, simply look at an icon (like Photos or Mail), and your headset will know you're looking there. Touch your index finger to your thumb to open it.

To close an app, look down below the open app and you'll see a white circle. When you look at that white circle, it turns into an X, which you can tap to close. Or just press the Digital Crown to go back to Home View.

Want to delete an app? Look at the app icon and tap and hold your index finger and thumb together. Apple Vision Pro will ask if you want to delete the app. Tap the X again, and the app will be uninstalled. Some apps, like Photos, can't be removed, so you won't see an option to delete it.

TIP

If you're about to delete an app and realize you don't want to, you can cancel the request by looking elsewhere on the screen and tapping your fingers.

Identifying the apps that come with Apple Vision Pro

Here's a list of the default apps in Apple Vision Pro and what they do:

>> **App Store:** The App Store is the digital store from which you can download new content (apps and games) to Apple Vision Pro. It's just like the App Store on your iPhone or iPad, except with apps specific to Apple Vision Pro.

>> **Books:** The Books app allows you to download and read e-books on Apple Vision Pro.

>> **Calendar:** The Calendar app enables you to keep track of events.

>> **Camera:** Use the Camera app to take photos and videos. You can also open the Camera app by pressing the top button over your left eye.

>> **Clock:** The Clock app includes a customizable world clock to see the time in various cities around the world. There are also an alarm, timer, and stopwatch.

>> **Contacts:** The Contacts app is an address book. You can select a person in your contacts and start a FaceTime video or audio call (or initiate a call from the People View).

>> **Files:** Open the Files app to access the files on your Apple Vision Pro.

>> **Freeform:** Freeform is a digital whiteboard where you can flesh out ideas. You can also use Freeform to collaborate with others in real time.

>> **Home:** The Home app enables you to access your compatible smart home products.

>> **Keynote:** The Keynote app is presentation software. If you're used to working on a Windows PC, Keynote is similar to Microsoft PowerPoint.

- >> **Mail:** The Mail app is where you read and write email messages while wearing Apple Vision Pro.

- >> **Maps:** The Maps app is — yep, you guessed it — where you can type in an address to see its location on a map, along with nearby businesses. You can also use it to get directions.

- >> **Messages:** The Messages app is where you send and receive iMessages (messages sent between Apple devices — you can identify them because the bubble they appear in is blue instead of green).

- >> **Mindfulness:** Take a break with calming exercises for the mind in the Mindfulness app.

- >> **Music:** Access your Apple Music library in the Music app.

- >> **News:** The News app takes you to Apple News, which curates content from leading publications.

- >> **Notes:** Create and view notes on Apple Vision Pro in the Notes app.

- >> **Photos:** View your library of photos and videos.

- >> **Podcasts:** Browse, search, listen to, and subscribe to millions of podcasts in the Podcasts app.

- >> **Reminders:** Set and view reminders you set for yourself in the Reminders app.

- >> **Safari:** Safari is Apple's own web browser (see Figure 4-2).

- >> **Shortcuts:** Create, view and change any shortcuts or automations you've used across your Apple devices in the Shortcuts app.

- >> **Stocks:** See stock prices for companies of your choosing and trends from popular stock indexes in the Stocks app.

- >> **Tips:** In the Tips app, Apple provides advice on how to get more out of your Apple Vision Pro.

- >> **TV:** Watch TV shows and movies from the Apple TV+ service (subscription required), sports (like MLS Season Pass), or anything you've purchased from Apple (even older iTunes content) in the TV app (shown in Figure 4-3).

- >> **Voice Memos:** Set voice notes for yourself, or record business meetings, classroom lectures, and more with the Voice Memos app.

Some apps may be in a subfolder called Compatible Apps, which you'll see in Home View. If you don't see any of the apps listed here installed on your Apple Vision Pro, the app may have been deleted (even accidentally), but you can download it again for free in the App Store.

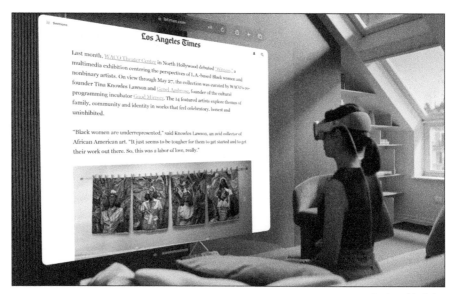

FIGURE 4-2:
Reading is surprisingly smooth on Apple Vision Pro, whether it's scrolling through articles on a website in Safari, shown here, or flipping through e-books.

Courtesy of Apple, Inc.

FIGURE 4-3:
MAX, one of the supported services inside the Apple TV app for Apple Vision Pro.

Courtesy of Apple, Inc.

REMEMBER

If you have the same app installed on another Apple device (like Books) it will automatically synchronize the app and its contents to Apple Vision Pro, unless you opted out of iCloud syncing on the other device.

Navigating the App Store

Just like the App Store for other Apple devices — iPhone, iPad, Apple Watch, Mac, and Apple TV+ — you can preview and download countless visionOS apps and games to use on your Apple Vision Pro. This lets you fully customize your experience with what matters to you.

TECHNICAL STUFF

At the time of writing, there were about 1,500 third-party (non-Apple) apps designed for Apple Vision Pro, or supported by Vision Pro (like many iPad apps), but expect that number to explode over the coming years.

Many compatible iPad and iPhone apps also work on Apple Vision Pro, including Amazon Prime Video, CNN, NBA, Reddit, Uber, and Uber Eats, to name few.

The following sections look at the App Store inside of Apple Vision Pro, and what you can see and do here.

Navigating the tab bar in the App Store

Just like Home View has a vertical tab bar to the left of the page (showing Apps, People, and Environments), the App Store has its own tab bar (see Figure 4-4) to the left of the storefront, also with three options:

>> **Apps & Games:** All the apps and games available for Apple Vision Pro users

>> **Apple Arcade:** For people who subscribe to the Apple Arcade service, which features hundreds of ad-free games (see Chapter 12)

>> **Search:** Enables you to search the App Store by keyword

The Apps & Games tab is selected by default. See Figure 4-4 for a look at the App Store tab bar in Apple Vision Pro.

Identifying the various sections of the App Store

Here's a look at some of the main sections of the App Store:

>> **Featured apps:** When you launch App Store, you'll first see the featured apps and games (or app collections) for that day, at the top of the screen. It will automatically scroll across to show you four or five featured apps or grouped apps, with some images and a brief description. This carousel is like the App Store for other devices. You may see a "From the Editors" (of the App Store) section, and there may be a themed collection of recommended apps, too.

Tab bar

FIGURE 4-4:
Toggle
between
Apps & Games,
Apple Arcade,
or Search.

Courtesy of Apple, Inc.

Pinch your index finger and thumb together, and scroll up to move down the page.

>> **What's New:** As the name says, these apps and games are new to the App Store. Here you'll see a few profiled apps, but you can also tap the small arrow (pointing right) beside the words *What's New* to see many more new apps to consider.

>> **Latest Stories:** This section of the App Store also contains curated app collections by App Store editors, including subsections like "What We Love," "Don't Miss," "Quick Tip," and more, for most of the themed app bundles (like "Essential Utilities" or "Experience the Ultimate Private Home Theater").

>> **Hot This Week:** In this section, the App Store will show you the most popular apps (based on number of downloads), so you can see what's trending.

>> **Browse By Category:** In this section, you'll see several categories of apps, such as "Entertainment Apps," "Education Apps," "Health & Fitness Apps," "Music Apps," and many others.

>> **For You:** This section looks at other apps you've downloaded to Apple Vision Pro or onto another Apple devices (signed into the same Apple ID) and suggests similar apps, based on your tastes. You may also see apps that you've downloaded onto another Apple device, like an iPhone.

- **》 Best Apps for Vision Pro:** This section is one more handpicked collection of apps from the App Store editors. The description for each app outlines why the editors think the app is worthy of your consideration.

- **》 Quick Links:** This last section includes links to additional information, based on the following:

  - About the App Store
  - About In-App Purchases
  - Report a Problem
  - Request a Refund

From time to time, you may see other sections in the App Store, like "Don't Miss" or "Try Now." Half the fun is discovering great new content on your own!

Knowing what info you'll see about each app

When you've tapped an app to learn more about it, you'll be able to see a ton of information about that app. On any app page, you'll find:

- **》** The name of the app, an icon for it, a one-sentence summary, and a full description

- **》** The price (whether it's free or the cost to download, in your local currency)

- **》** The star rating (out of 5) and how many people rated it

- **》** Customer comments from people who have previously downloaded the app (and maybe the developer's response underneath)

- **》** The recommended age rating for the app and why (for example, "Age rating 17+ Years Old for Cigarette/Alcohol and Drug Use, Partial Nudity," and so on)

- **》** The app category (such as "Graphics and Design")

- **》** The developer (either a person or a company) that made or published the app

- **》** Screenshots of the app (and maybe a short video loop or animation) of the app in action

- **》** What's new (if the app has been updated)

- **》** App privacy information (such as whether data is collected from users, and if so, what kind of data)

- **》** The size of the app

- **》** The language the app uses

- >> The app's compatibility (for example, will say "Works on this Vision Pro")

- >> If there are any in-app purchases (optional) and how much they cost

- >> A link to the developer's website

- >> Other apps sold by the developer

- >> A Share button, which enables you to share a link to the app with someone

Buying apps

Ready to buy an app? It's simple. For any app you want to download, tap the Get button (which means it's free; see Figure 4-5) or tap the price (such as $2.99) to buy the app. You'll be prompted to double-click the Digital Crown (above your right eye) to confirm you want to download the app.

FIGURE 4-5: Because it says "Get" where the price would normally be, this means this Sky Guide astronomy app is free to download.

Courtesy of Marc Saltzman

REMEMBER

When you set up Apple Vision Pro for the first time, you were asked to add payment information for buying new apps. If you didn't complete that step, you'll be asked to add your payment information, which you can also do by opening the Settings app, tapping your name, tapping Payment & Shipping, and tapping Add Payment Method. You'll see your balance (if you have any credit left on your account), as well as credit and debit cards and maybe PayPal (in the United States and Canada).

If you change your mind and don't want to download the app, tap the X to get out of the payment section.

When you tap to download an app, you'll see a white circle start to rotate around the app icon, clockwise, which should give you an indication of how long it'll take to download over Wi-Fi to your device. When the ring around the circle completes, you'll hear a short tone to confirm the app has been downloaded, and you'll be able to find the app icon in Home View.

TIP

Apple Vision Pro will know if you don't have enough storage to download the app. You many need to remove some existing apps to make room for the new one. At any time, you can open the Settings app and tap Storage to see what apps are taking up the most space and decide what to do from there.

Contacting Friends, Family, or Whoever You Want

When you tap the People tab in Home View, you see icons for a couple of people you've communicated with previously and/or often. You also see their photos or Memojis (cartoon representations of people) or initials in a circle above their names. Figure 4-6 shows some examples.

If you tap one of these icons, you can choose whether to message or call them, send an email, engage in a FaceTime call, and more. Tapping the three dots opens up your options.

Click Info to read more about that person, including their Contacts card, any media you may have shared with each other, the date of your last correspondence, and more.

You can also tap the plus sign (+)to the left of the People tab to initiate communication with someone in a variety of ways, like FaceTime.

Finally, you can pin a favorite contact to your People tab, so they'll always appear there.

FIGURE 4-6:
Launching the
People tab
on the Home
View screen,
brings up icons
of people
you've recently
communicated
with.

Viewing and Changing Environments

Environments are sort of like wallpaper, except they can transport you to a different scenic place on earth (such as Yosemite, Joshua Tree, or Mount Hood) or even outside the Earth (the Moon is an option, too). There are also colored Environments that aren't based on a real location, such as Summer Light, Winter Light, Fall Light, Spring Light, or Morning Light.

You can add Environments to your view in Apple Vision Pro, whether you're in Home View or accessing apps like Safari, Mail, and others.

TIP

Some apps have exclusive Environments that are available only in that app, such as a virtual Conference Room to rehearse a Keynote presentation.

Environments are a fun way to dress up your view in Apple Vision Pro, and they're easy to launch and change. You can adjust the scope of the visual and audio impact of your Environment, too.

Choosing an Environment

There are a few ways to choose an Environment.

>> From Home View, tap Environments in the tab bar on the left and select one.

>> Open the Settings app, and then tap Environments.

>> Ask Siri to launch Environments. For example, say, "Siri, take me to the Moon" or "Siri, take me to Haleakalā." See below for more on using Siri for Environments.

Change the appearance and volume in Environments

You can choose whether you want your Environment to be light or dark, or stretch all around you — so even if you look over your shoulder, you'll still see the wraparound image. Apple calls this visual effect *immersion,* and it's shown in Figure 4-7.

For light or dark, open Control Center, tap the Environments button, and then tap Light, Dark, or Automatic.

TIP

The light and dark options don't apply to the light-based Environments (Summer Light, Winter Light, Fall Light, Spring Light, and Morning Light).

To adjust the level of immersion (how much the Environment takes up your field of view), turn the Digital Crown (above your right eye). Turning the Digital Crown back and forth adjusts the amount of immersion. Depending on what you're doing in Apple Vision Pro, you may need to look at the Environments icon first (near the top of your view) while you turn the Digital Crown.

You may hear effects in Environments, like wind blowing at Yosemite or rain droplets on the water in Mount Hood, and some birds chirping, faintly, as well. Some of these effects are available only if you don't have apps open.

TIP

To adjust the volume of Environment sounds, do one of the following:

FIGURE 4-7: On the top, you see the Environments screen with a few options to choose from. On the bottom, you see the White Sands option in Environments, which I chose to wrap around to cover my entire view (even if I looked left and right).

Top: Courtesy of Apple, Inc.; Bottom: Courtesy of Marc Saltzman

>> When you're in an Environment, look near the upper right of the screen for some settings to appear, look at the volume level, and turn the Digital Crown left or right (for volume up or down, respectively).

>> Open Control Center, tap the Volume button, and pinch and drag the volume slider left or right.

To quickly switch between your surroundings and immersion, double-tap the Digital Crown to see your surroundings. To return to your Environment, press the Digital Crown once.

When you have an Environment open, you can also see people through Apple Vision Pro when they approach you.

REMEMBER

If you move out from the boundary — the physical area you're in while wearing Apple Vision Pro — the immersive experience gradually fades to reveal your surroundings (say, if you walk across the room). When you return to the original position or recenter your view, the Environment experience returns to the previous immersion level.

Using Siri with Environments

In addition to using Siri to open an Environment, you can call upon your personal assistant for help with Environments. For example, ask Siri any of the following:

>> "Siri, what Environments do I have?"

>> "Siri, turn off my Environment."

>> "Siri, make it daytime."

You can also look at an Environment when all the icons are presented on the screen and say, "Siri, open this Environment."

Perusing a list of the Environments that are available (so far)

More Environments are released all the time, but Table 4-1 lists the ones that were in place as I was writing this book.

TABLE 4-1 **Available Environments**

Built-in into Apple Vision Pro	When in Specific Apps
Haleakala	Conference Room (Keynote)
Yosemite	Steve Jobs Theater (Keynote)
Joshua Tree	Game of Thrones Theater (MAX)
Mount Hood	Disney Theater (Disney+)
Moon	Scare Factory (Disney+)
White Sands	Avenger's Tower (Disney+)
ATV+ (Apple TV+) Theater	Tatooine from Star Wars (Disney+)

TIP

While you're having fun using Apple Vision Pro, know that the battery pack will only last up to 2.5 hours (or less, if you're engaged in a game or other app that's more taxing on the device's power). Since there's no easy way to see your battery level without looking all the way up and pinching open the Control Center, consider downloading a free (or at least cheap) app that gives you a persistent onscreen view of your battery. At the App Store, search for "clock" or "battery." One popular pick is a $2 (USD) one called Battery Saver Widget app.

Chapter 5

Accessing and Changing Your Apple Vision Pro Settings

J ust as with all your consumer electronics — from your TV and smartphone to your e-reader and laptop — you can view and adjust multiple settings on your Apple Vision Pro so you can customize it to your exact needs.

The Settings app lets you browse by section or search for settings you want to change, such as your Wi-Fi network, passcode, Environment settings (see Chapter 4), font size, and more.

TIP

Don't worry about damaging your headset with anything you change in Settings — everything can be reversed if you need to.

This chapter walks you through all the options you have via the Settings app in Apple Vision Pro.

Opening the Settings App

To open the Settings app, do either of the following:

➤ Press the Digital Crown to open Home View. You should see your apps, as shown in Figure 5-1. (If you don't, look at the tab bar on the left, and then tap Apps.) Tap the Settings icon, which looks like a gray gear.

➤ If enabled, use Siri to access Settings. Simply say, "Siri, open Settings."

FIGURE 5-1: As with all Apple devices, the Settings icon looks like a gray gear.

Courtesy of Apple, Inc.

That's all there is to it.

Using the Settings App

When you open the Settings app, you'll see either the last section you were in or the main Settings page. Either way, how you navigate through the various options will be the same. You have three options:

➤ Scroll through the main category of settings on the left, and tap the one you want to view and/or change.

» Tap the Search field (in the upper left of the screen), enter a word or two (for example, "brightness"), and then tap the setting you're looking for in the search results.

» Tap the Search field and then look at the Dictation button, which looks like a microphone, to the left of the Search field. Say out loud what you're looking for instead of typing it. Then tap the setting you're looking for in the search results.

REMEMBER

Again, all Settings categories are listed along the left-hand side of the Settings app. You can scroll up and down by pinching your index finger and thumb together and dragging up and down. To select a Settings category, look at the word and tap to open the options on the right-hand side of the screen.

Viewing and Changing Settings Options

The main Settings options are listed vertically, down the entire left side of the screen (see Figure 5-2). Here they are:

» **Your name and Apple ID:** You'll see this at the top of the screen, represented by your profile photo, your Memoji, or another image, along with your name and Apple ID. Tap your name to see all your personal info, including your passcode, payment and shipping info, subscriptions, iCloud storage amount, the Apple devices you own, and more.

FIGURE 5-2:
The main view of the Settings app, where you have several dozen settings to view and change as you see fit.

Courtesy of Apple, Inc.

>> **Wi-Fi:** Tap Wi-Fi to see a list of the nearby Wi-Fi networks, what network you're signed into, hotspot info (if you want to connect to a smartphone for internet access), and more.

>> **Bluetooth:** If Bluetooth wireless is enabled, tap Bluetooth to see what devices your Apple Vision Pro is connected to via Bluetooth (for example, your AirPods).

>> **General:** Apple lumps a bunch of settings in this section, which includes updating your Apple Vison Pro, AppleCare and warranty info, whether AirDrop is on (to wirelessly send media to nearby Apple devices), storage, date and time settings, keyboard and fonts, and more.

>> **Apps:** Tap Apps to see all the apps you have installed, listed alphabetically (or maybe in the Compatible Apps subfolder near the bottom of the screen). Look at and then tap to open an app's settings, and you'll have many options here. For example, if you tap Mail, you can choose what your default email app is, all the accounts you've set up inside of it (if you have multiple email addresses), swipe options, adding carbon copy (CC) or blind carbon copy (BCC) recipients, how your messages should be organized, signatures (at the end of your email messages), and more.

>> **People:** Tap People to look at the people (Contacts) you have associated with your Apple ID. You can choose the sort order, review or update your own personal info, see blocked contacts, and more.

>> **Environments:** Environments are optional visual (and sometimes audible) ways to spice up your Apple Vision Pro experience. Tap Environments to adjust the appearance (light, dark, or automatic) or volume. (See Chapter 4 for more on Environments.)

>> **Notifications:** Tap Notifications to control whether you want an app to notify you of something — for example, when a new email message is waiting for you or when a bonus level is added to your favorite game. You can enable or disable notifications for each of your apps here, and also select what to be notified about specifically for each app.

>> **Sounds:** Tap Sounds to adjust the volume of your ringtone and alerts, as well as headphone audio settings.

>> **Focus:** Based on what you're doing while wearing Apple Vision Pro, you can choose to not be disturbed, what times of the day or evening you don't want to be disturbed, set up Mindfulness exercises to serve as little mental health breaks during a workday, and more.

>> **Screen Time:** Tap Screen Time to see what apps you're looking at and for how long. Here you can also set up a passcode to secure Screen Time settings.

>> **FaceTime:** Tap FaceTime to enable or disable FaceTime, what Apple ID it's associated with, and more.

>> **Persona:** Tap Persona to see what your Persona looks like (see Chapter 2), including details you can edit, recapturing options, and more. (***Note:*** At the time of writing this book, Persona was in beta, meaning the software was still being tested and not an official feature just yet.)

>> **Eyes & Hands:** This part of Settings lets you redo eye and hand setup in Apple Vision Pro and make various adjustments, too.

>> **People Awareness:** People Awareness shows people nearby. Visibility depends on your settings, motion, and their distance. You can make passthrough and EyeSight changes here (see Chapter 3).

>> **Accessibility:** Covered extensively in Chapter 3, this big part of Settings lets you select and tweak all kinds of accessibility settings.

>> **Control Center:** Tap Control Center to select various options related to — you guessed it! — the Control Center. For example, you can change the position of the Control Center (including how high or low it appears when you look up) and add or remove special accessibility aids.

>> **Siri & Search:** Here you can enable Siri to listen for you (by saying "Siri" or "Hey Siri"), change Siri's voice, select whether you want to hear or read Siri's response, and more.

>> **Privacy & Security:** You have many options tied to your own privacy when using Apple Vision Pro and its many apps. Tap Privacy & Security to preview and/or change these options.

>> **Display:** Tap Display to tweak things like text size, brightness, display appearance, window zoom size, and more.

>> **Battery:** Tap this to see the battery percentage while you're using Apple Vision Pro (or to hide the battery percentage).

>> **Storage:** Tap Storage to access your Apple Vision Pro's storage area (which you can also find by tapping your name at the top of the Settings screen) and see how much storage you've used, see the storage requirements per app, set whether you want to offload the app, and more.

TECHNICAL STUFF

Offloading an app doesn't officially delete it. It frees up memory on your device while keeping some of the app data (such as your progress in a game). If the app is still available in the App Store, your content is accessible after the app is re-downloaded to the device.

>> **Optic ID & Passcode:** After you type in your PIN you can see the settings for your Optic ID and what it unlocks by looking at your irises. You can also

change your PIN and adjust your password autofill options, Wallet and Apple Pay settings, and more.

» **Passwords:** The Passwords app, which you unlock using Optic ID, lets you see your passwords and passkeys for each app. Tap Passwords to set when and how the Passwords app is used, and find out if Apple has detected any security concerns (for example, if a data breach revealed one of your used passwords).

» **Game Center:** If you play games and you're part of the Game Center community of Apple users, this is where you see your profile information and can make changes to your name, avatar, and more.

» **TV Provider:** If you add your TV provider from the list of options, you may be able to watch TV shows and movies from apps included in your TV subscription. (See Chapter 9 for more.)

» **Wallet & Apple Pay:** Tap Wallet & Apple to view and change your digital wallet info and cards, shipping info, and more. These settings are also accessible in the Optic ID & Passcode section, mentioned earlier.

REMEMBER

Any time you want to get out of the Settings app, simply look to the bottom of the screen and stare for a moment at the white dot to the left. The white dot will turn into an X, which you can tap to close the app.

2

Using Apple Vision Pro to Communicate

IN THIS PART . . .

Master all the ways you can use Apple Vision Pro to keep in touch with those who matter.

Send and receive iMessages with Apple Vision Pro.

Read and respond to emails in Apple Vision Pro, including typing on a virtual keyboard or by using your voice.

Make audio and video calls using Apple Vision Pro, including FaceTime chats using your custom Persona.

Chapter **6**
Making FaceTime Calls

The versatile Apple Vision Pro has so many uses, and video communication is one of them. Sure, you can use another Apple device — like an iPhone or Mac — to FaceTime, but doing so hands-free on an Apple Vision Pro is really engaging because you can pin the people you're chatting with around the actual room you're in. Plus, you look almost 3D to the people you're chatting with, thanks to your Persona (see Chapter 2).

During a FaceTime video call, you can also share your view with the person you're chatting with, so they see what you see. Plus, you can add more people to the call, message them during a call, pin multiple faces around the environment you're in (see Figure 6-1), and much more.

Several Apple Vision Pro apps even let you video chat while doing something online, such as playing chess with a friend in another city (see Chapter 12) or collaborating with a colleague in Freeform (see Chapter 16). This is part of the SharePlay feature is baked into Apple Vision Pro (and some other Apple devices).

In this chapter, I explain how to conduct a FaceTime call and how to share your hologram-like Persona during an app or game.

TIP

If you haven't set up your Persona yet, turn to Chapter 2 to do that first.

FIGURE 6-1:
On Apple
Vision Pro, you
can FaceTime
with multiple
people at once
in various
windows
pinned around
your space.

Courtesy of Apple, Inc.

Starting a FaceTime Call

To start a FaceTime call using Apple Vision Pro, follow these steps:

1. **In Home View, tap People in the tab bar on the left (see Figure 6-2).**

2. **Tap the plus (+) symbol.**

3. **Tap New FaceTime.**

4. **Type the name, number, or email address you want to call.**

   You can call multiple people at once (up to 32 people).

5. **Tap the FaceTime button to make a video call or the Audio Call button to make an audio call.**

   Alternatively, tap and hold on a face in you People video and select FaceTime call (see Figure 6-3).

TIP

In the Messages app, you can start a FaceTime call with someone right from a conversation — just tap the FaceTime button at the upper right of the Messages conversation, and tap FaceTime Video or FaceTime Audio.

If a FaceTime call comes in while you're wearing Apple Vision Pro, you'll hear the familiar ring and see the FaceTime icon at the top of your view. Tap to select it, and then tap Join. You can also tap the word *Join* under the contact in People View. Too busy? Not feeling social? To reject the call, tap Dismiss.

FIGURE 6-2:
Tap People in the tab bar on the left.

Courtesy of Apple, Inc.

FIGURE 6-3:
Tap and hold on someone (like my daughter Maya, shown here) and choose to FaceTime them from the list of options.

Courtesy of Marc Saltzman

CREATING A LINK TO A FACETIME CALL

Instead of initiating a FaceTime call, you can create a link to a FaceTime call and send it to one person or to a group of people. They can then use that link to join or start a FaceTime call with you. This feature is handy if you're setting up a call in the future, as a calendar entry, or if the person you want to FaceTime with isn't on an Apple device.

Here's how to do it:

1. **In Home View, tap People in the tab bar on the left.**
2. **Tap the New FaceTime button.**
3. **Tap Create Link.**
4. **Choose an option for sending the link (for example, Message, Calendar, or Mail), or tap Copy.**

    You can also add a name to the link, such as the name of a meeting or event.

In the Calendar app, you can schedule a remote video meeting by inserting FaceTime as the location of the meeting.

During a FaceTime Call: Moving People, Using Apps, Sharing Views, and More

Once you're engaged in a FaceTime call, you can do any of the following:

>> **Move faces around.** If you want to move someone's face to a different part of your room, look at the horizontal bar below the FaceTime window, pinch your index finger and thumb together, move the window somewhere, and open your fingers to pin them there.

>> **Enlarge or shrink the People view.** Just as you can drag and drop people's faces around to pin them to your real space, you can also make each person's view bigger or smaller. Simply look at the person you're chatting with, and you'll see a white curve in the lower right of their window, which means you can pinch your index finger and thumb together and pull out and in to make the window bigger or smaller.

>> **Add more people.** To add more participants to the FaceTime call, tap the name, number, or email of the person you're talking to at the bottom of the FaceTime window. If you don't see the call controls, tap the FaceTime window

to bring it up. Tap Add People, and then choose a contact or enter someone's contact information. Then tap Invite.

» **Send a message to people on the call.** If you want to message someone you're chatting with — for example, sending them an address to meet up later — tap the name, number, or email of the person or group you're talking to at the bottom of the FaceTime window. If you don't see the call controls, tap the FaceTime window. Tap Info. Then tap Message to type your note.

» **Use other apps.** Like multitasking? During a FaceTime call, you can continue working in your apps, such as browsing the web, reading email, or jotting down a shopping list in the Notes app. If the apps you're in aren't meant to be shared with people in the call, there will be a label at the top of the window that says "Not Shared." If you want others to be able to follow along with what you're doing, you can share your view.

» **Share your view (or a window in your view).** If you want those you're chatting with over FaceTime to see what you're doing, you can share your view or a window in your view.

To share your entire view, tap the Share View button. Others on the call will see your entire view, including your Environment or your physical surroundings. Choose an Environment if you don't want them to see the room you're in (see Chapter 4).

To share a window, tap Not Shared above the window, and then tap Share My Entire Window.

» **Use Siri during a call.** When you use Siri during a FaceTime call, others on the call will hear your request, like "What's the weather like today in Miami?" but they won't hear Siri's response. To share a window with others on the call, look at the app and say something like "Siri, share this."

» **Turn off audio.** To mute yourself, tap the Mute button. Tap again to unmute.

» **Turn off your Persona.** Feeling shy? To hide your Persona during a call, tap the Persona button. Tap it again to show your Persona.

FaceTiming with SharePlay on Apple Vision Pro

Apple Vision Pro users can watch TV shows and movies, listen to music, and play games with other people who are not there with them physically, all by placing a FaceTime call! Pretty amazing.

This feature, aptly named SharePlay, lets you consume content at the same time as other people, while also enjoying a real-time chat if you like. What's more, playback of this streamed content is synchronized between users, and with shared controls, you see and hear the same big moments together at the same time.

When you open an app that supports SharePlay during a FaceTime call, like Music, a message will temporarily appear above the app to indicate that it supports SharePlay (or that it can start using SharePlay automatically).

Some SharePlay-supported apps, such as Apple TV+, require a subscription, so all participants will need to have an account in order to view that content. In other words, you can't be an Apple TV+ subscriber yourself and SharePlay the new episode of *The Morning Show* with your friend who doesn't pay for an Apple TV+ subscription. (Nothing's stopping you from inviting that friend over to sit in your living room and watch it with you, though!)

To SharePlay content with others in FaceTime, follow these steps:

1. **Start a FaceTime call.**

2. **Open Home View to see your apps.**

3. **Launch a streaming app that supports SharePlay, like Music or Apple TV.**

4. **Select what you want to watch or listen to, tap the Play button, and select SharePlay to begin watching or listening with everyone on the call.**

   Others on the call may have to tap Join SharePlay on their own devices.

TIP

Each person can use the playback controls to play, pause, rewind, or fast-forward for the entire group. But some settings, like closed captioning and volume, are controlled separately by each person — so, for example, if your parents want to turn up the volume on their devices, it won't turn up the volume for your brother with the sleeping baby in the next room.

If you're listening to tunes in Music, anyone using SharePlay can add songs to the shared queue — and they don't need a subscription to Apple Music to tune in, as opposed to some other SharePlay experiences (like Apple TV+), where all parties on the call need a subscription.

You can FaceTime with others while inside a SharePlay-supported app, so you can see them and work (or watch) together at the same time (see Figure 6-4). If the person you're chatting with is wearing Apple Vision Pro, you'll see their hologram-like spatial Persona (see Figure 6-5).

FIGURE 6-4:
A SharePlay-
supported
chat, where
the Apple
Vision Pro
wearer sees
two colleagues
while working
on a project.

Courtesy of Apple, Inc.

FIGURE 6-5:
Two people
discussing
a Freeform
board.

Courtesy of Apple, Inc.

You can also start a FaceTime call from a compatible music or video app, and then SharePlay from there:

1. **Open an app that supports SharePlay, such as Apple TV or Music.**

2. **Tap a show, movie, or song you want to share, tap the Share button, and tap SharePlay.**

   In some apps, you may need to first tap More and then tap Share.

3. In the To field, enter the contacts you want to share with, and then tap FaceTime.

4. After the FaceTime call connects, tap Start or Play to begin using SharePlay.

TIP

You can also play games with people during a FaceTime call. Some multiplayer games can be played with friends in Game Center — an Apple service that allows users to play and challenge friends when playing online — while wearing Apple Vision Pro. You have to set up your Game Center profile first. Open the Settings app, tap Game Center, tap Invite Friends, and then find and download a supported multiplayer game for Game Center in the App Store. During a FaceTime call, open the game, tap Start SharePlay, and then follow the onscreen instructions.

Trying Out Spatial Personas on Apple Vision Pro

If you thought SharePlay in FaceTime was cool, wait 'til you get a load of spatial Personas with SharePlay! Spatial Personas on Apple Vision Pro is an exciting way to interact with others in a virtual environment.

Supporting up to five people, spatial Personas lets you see a hologram-like view of the person (or people) you're on a FaceTime call with, seemingly floating in the real environment you're in. There's even support for gesturing with hands, too. You can enable spatial Personas while collaborating in a Freeform brainstorming session (digital whiteboarding), while watching a movie together, or while playing a compatible multiplayer game.

Not only can you virtually see other Apple Vision Pro users while in an app together, but you and others can even point and interact with the content in this mixed-reality space. For example, three or four colleagues can look at and draw and write on the same Freeform board (see Chapter 16) and intermittently make eye contact, too.

What's more, by folding in Spatial Audio technology, the voices seemingly come from the direction of the people talking, so it really feels like you're together in the same room.

REMEMBER

Spatial Personas are still in beta at the time of this writing, so it may not be an official feature when you're reading this book.

To launch spatial Personas, follow these steps:

1. **During a FaceTime call, tap the Spatial button at the bottom of the screen.**

   At least one other person on the call must also tap the Spatial button for this special hologram-like floating view. Those who don't tap the Spatial button (or aren't using Apple Vision Pro) will stay as a tile in your view (like a regular FaceTime call).

2. **To reposition a Persona in your space, look at the Persona, and then pinch and drag it.**

The position of Personas will change depending on what you're doing in the call. For instance, a Persona will appear next to you, as if you were sitting beside one another in a movie theater, if you're watching a movie together in SharePlay. But if you're playing a game together in SharePlay, a Persona may appear across from you.

LINKING YOUR IPHONE TO HAND OFF CALLS

Another way to make phone calls while wearing Apple Vision Pro is for iPhone owners to enable Handoff calls on other Apple devices. On your iPhone, open the Settings app, tap Phone, tap Calls on Other Devices, and enable Apple Vision Pro in the list.

If you don't see your Apple Vision Pro on the list, make sure that you're signed into the same Apple ID on both devices, you've got Wi-Fi Calling enabled, and you're on the same Wi-Fi network as your other devices.

Now, whenever a call comes in, you can choose to answer it on your Apple Vision Pro, Mac, iPad, or other Apple product you're on, by tapping the green Accept call icon.

IN THIS CHAPTER

» Getting ready to use the iMessage
  option

» Writing and replying to messages

» Sending your name and photo

» Adjusting the notifications for the
  Messages app

Chapter **7**

Sending and Receiving Messages

A s with most other Apple products — including iPhone, iPad, Mac, and Apple
Watch — you can easily keep in touch with people using Apple Vision Pro.
The Messages app may not be as slick as FaceTime (see Chapter 6), but you
can easily send, read, and respond to messages inside of your new mixed-reality
headset (see Figure 7-1).

TIP

Messages are handled through the built-in Messages app, which lets you exchange
messages over Wi-Fi with people who also use Apple's proprietary iMessage feature on an Apple device. iMessage texts appear in blue bubbles, as opposed to
the green bubbles used for regular text messages (if you have an iPhone, you're
familiar with this experience). Unlike on an iPhone, however, on Apple Vision Pro,
you can only communicate via iMessage with other Apple users — you can't send
text messages to non-Apple users.

This chapter covers how to sign in and use iMessages in Apple Vision Pro, how to
text with one or more people, and how to adjust the kinds of notifications you get
inside the headset.

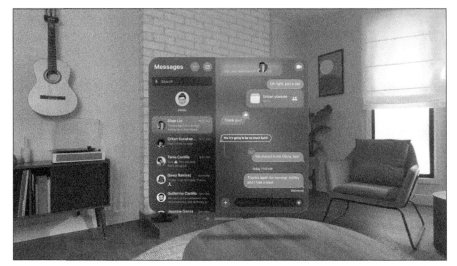

FIGURE 7-1:
In Apple Vision
Pro, you
see a huge
chat window
hovering in
the air in front
of you.

Turning on iMessage

If you didn't do this when you first set up your Apple Vision Pro (see Chapter 2), the first step is to ensure you're signed in using your Apple ID and turned on iMessage. Just follow these steps:

1. **While wearing your Apple Vision Pro, open the Settings app, and tap Apps, tap Messages, and turn on iMessage.**

2. **To select the phone numbers and email addresses you want to use with iMessage, tap Send & Receive.**

    Under You Can Receive iMessages to and Reply From, you should see the email address associated with your Apple ID, as well as possibly your phone number.

3. **Choose how you want to be messaged.**

When you use iMessage on your Apple Vision Pro, your messages are kept up to date, backed up, and synchronized among all your Apple devices — as long as you've enabled Messages in iCloud and you're signed in with the same Apple ID on those devices. In other words, all your conversations show up automatically in the Messages app, regardless of which device you're on. In fact, after you turn on Messages in iCloud, any messages or attachments you delete from Apple Vision Pro are also deleted from your other Apple devices (iPhone, iPad, Apple Watch, and Mac) where Messages in iCloud is turned on.

REMEMBER

Messages in iCloud uses up iCloud storage. If you run out of storage space, you'll need to remove content or decide to pay for a monthly iCloud+ subscription for additional data. In the United States, prices start at $0.99 per month for 50GB of data. You can find more info at `https://support.apple.com/en-us/108047`.

To turn on Messages in iCloud:

1. **Open the Settings app, tap your name, tap iCloud, and tap Show All.**
2. **Enable Messages in iCloud.**

Sending and Responding to Messages

After you've turned on iMessage on your Apple Vision Pro, you can send messages while wearing the device, as well as read and reply to messages that come in.

To get going, follow these steps:

1. **From Home View, look at the green Messages app.**

   If you have messages waiting to be read, you'll see a small number in a red notification bubble in the upper right of the app icon to indicate how many unread messages you have.

2. **Tap the tip of your index finger with your thumb to open Messages.**

   You see your most recent conversations to the left.

3. **To continue chatting with someone you've recently chatted with, tap their name.**

   A virtual keyboard appears in front of you.

4. **To start a fresh conversation, tap the Compose icon (it looks like a square with an arrow coming out of the top).**

   A virtual keyboard appears in front of you.

   If the person you want to send a message to is already in your Contacts, start typing their name, phone number, or email address. The To field will become populated with their name. Click to confirm this is who you want to write to.

   If the person you want to send a message to is not in your Contacts, finish typing their phone number or email address.

You can only send iMessages on Apple Vision Pro, so the phone number or email address you enter must be set up to receive iMessages — if the person you're trying to reach isn't on an Apple device or hasn't set up to receive iMessages with that phone number or email address, you're out of luck. For example, if you type in a phone number or email address of someone without iMessage support (maybe a friend on an Android device), you won't be able to even send the message because the Send arrow will be grayed out.

5. **To add one or more additional recipients to the same message, click the + (plus) symbol to the right of the To field and start typing the new name, number, or email address.**

   The new recipients are listed beside the first one.

6. **Type your message.**

   You can move the virtual keyboard around by looking below the keyboard at the horizontal white bar, pressing and holding it (by pinching your index finger with your thumb), and then moving the keyboard somewhere else and letting go.

   You can use a Bluetooth keyboard if you prefer. And you can also tap the microphone icon to dictate the message you want to send and your words will be transcribed.

   Don't forget: You can dress up your messages by adding emojis, as shown in Figure 7-2. Just tap the emoji button on the lower left of the keyboard (it looks like a smiley face).

FIGURE 7-2: Add emojis for fun!

Courtesy of Marc Saltzman

7. **When you're done writing your message, send it by tapping the blue up-arrow icon inside your message field.**

   You'll hear a "whisked away" sound to indicate that the message has been sent.

8. **To close the Messages app, look below the app screen and focus your eyes on the white dot; after the white dot turns into an X, tap your index finger and thumb together.**

Sharing Your Name and Photo with the People You Message

Just as you can in the Messages app on iPhone, iPad and Mac, you can share your name and photo whenever you send or receive a message from someone new. You can also edit your name, photo, and sharing options. Follow these steps:

1. **Open the Messages app, look at the conversation list on the left, and tap the More button (the icon with the three dots) in the upper-left corner.**

2. **Tap Set up Name and Photo (if you haven't already done this) or tap Edit Name and Photo (if you've done this before).**

3. **To add or change your picture, tap Edit Photo below the circle, and then choose an option.**

   You can add a filter to your photo if you want.

4. **To add or edit your name, tap the text fields where your name appears.**

5. **You can choose to share your name and image automatically with Contacts Only or Always Ask (with the latter, you'll be prompted before this information is shared).**

Tweaking Notifications for Messages

You can customize how you want to be notified of incoming messages when wearing your Apple Vision Pro. From Home View, open the Settings app, tap Notifications, and tap Messages. Now change any of the following settings as you see fit:

» **Allow Notifications:** If you want to be notified of messages while wearing Apple Vision Pro, turn this on.

>> **Always Deliver Immediately:** If you want to receive time-sensitive notifications, even if you're in Focus mode (for example, Do Not Disturb), turn this on.

>> **Notification Center:** In the Alerts section, tap the Notification Center check box if you want to see alerts in the Notification Center.

>> **Banners:** In the Alerts section, tap the Banners check box if you want to see messages as a horizontal banner in front of you.

>> **Banner Style:** If you selected the Banners check box, you'll see a Banner Style setting. You can choose Temporary (to have the banner disappear shortly after popping up) or Persistent (to have the banner remain until you dismiss it).

>> **Sounds:** Tap Sounds to select the sound you want to hear when a message comes in.

>> **Badges:** If you want to see how many messages are waiting for you as a badge on the Messages app icon in Home View, turn on the Badges option.

>> **Notification Grouping:** Tap this to choose if you want notifications from the Messages app to be grouped automatically, by app, or not at all.

IN THIS CHAPTER

» Adding and removing email accounts in the Mail app

» Checking your email

» Composing and sending email

» Organizing your emails

» Tweaking your settings in Mail

» Searching for an email

Chapter **8**

Reading, Writing, and Managing Email

Whether you love email or hate it, it's a part of many people's daily lives.

In this chapter, I show you how to set up your email accounts in Apple Vision Pro using the built-in Mail app.

There are also third-party mail apps for Apple Vision Pro (like Airmail) or you can access Gmail or Outlook using Mac Virtual Display (see Chapter 16), but this chapter focuses on the default app that's already included, which is Apple's own Mail program (and hey, it works well, too!). I show you how to draft a message, read and respond to incoming emails, organize your mail, searching for something in particular, and more.

Setting Up Your Email Accounts in the Mail App

Before you can start sending and receiving emails on your Apple Vision Pro, you need to set up your email accounts in the Mail app.

TECHNICAL STUFF

At the time of writing this book, the only other email app supported in Apple Vision Pro was one called Airmail, but more will be coming, no doubt, as the headset becomes more popular.

Here's how to set up an email address in the Mail app:

1. **From the main Home View screen, look at the Mail app and open it by pinching your index finger to your thumb.**

   If this is your first time opening the app, you may be asked to set up an email account; if so simply follow the instructions. If you see your email messages, you've already set up at least one account (likely, the one connected to your Apple ID).

2. **To add another email account, open the Settings app, tap Apps, tap Mail, tap Accounts, and tap Add Account.**

3. **Tap one of the email services listed (for example, iCloud, Gmail, Yahoo!, and so on), and then enter your email account information.**

   If your email isn't affiliated with one of the services listed, tap Other, tap Add Mail Account, and then enter your email account information.

4. **To exit out of the Settings app, look at the bottom of the screen toward the little white circle on the left; when it turns into an X, click the X.**

TECHNICAL STUFF

By default, *push* email will be selected for all your mail accounts, which means the messages will appear as often as they come in, as opposed to your having to *pull* down email from the server. If you want to switch from push to pull, you can do so in the Settings app by tapping Apps, tapping Mail, tapping Accounts, and selecting the Fetch New Data switch at the bottom.

To remove email accounts, open the Settings app, tap Mail, tap Accounts, tap the email account you want to remove, and then do one of the following:

>> **If you're removing an iCloud email account,** tap iCloud, tap iCloud Mail, and then turn off Use on This Apple Vision Pro.

>> **If you're removing another email account,** turn off Mail. If you want to completely remove that email account from any app accessing it on Apple Vision Pro (not just turn off messages), tap Delete Account.

Reading Your Email

A badge in the upper-right corner of the app will tell you how many unread messages are waiting for you. Here's how to check email on your Apple Vision Pro:

1. **From the main Home View screen, look at the Mail app and open it by pinching your index finger to your thumb.**

2. **Click Inbox on the left-hand side and select a message.**

    The contents/body of the email are on the right-hand side (see Figure 8-1).

FIGURE 8-1: Here's what email messages look like while wearing Apple Vision Pro.

ADDING A CONTACT INSIDE THE MAIL APP

To add Contacts directly in the Mail app, to the right of a person's name or email address, tap their name again, and then select Create New Contact or Add to Existing Contact. You can add a phone number, other email addresses, and more.

Getting notified of new email messages

To be notified whenever new emails come in, you can tweak the notification settings by opening the Settings app, tapping Notifications, tapping Mail, and tapping Allow Notifications. Select Banner if you want to see the notification bubble at the top of whatever you're doing, tap Sounds and select whether you want a sound to play when an email arrives, and more. Figure 8-2 shows an example of your options.

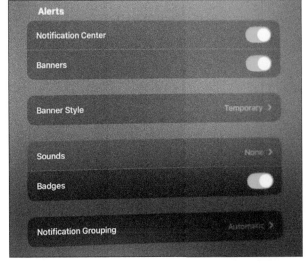

FIGURE 8-2:
You can adjust how to be notified when new emails come in while wearing Apple Vision Pro.

Setting email reminders in the Mail app

If you don't have time to respond to an email right away, you can set a time and date to receive a reminder and bring a message back to the top of your inbox. It's completely optional, but some people like the reminder. Swipe left on a message, tap the More button (it looks like three dots), tap Remind Me (see Figure 8-3), and then choose when to be reminded. You can also flag a message as important, delete it, and more.

Previewing an email message

If you want to see what an email is about but not open it completely, you can see a few words under the name of the recipient, as a preview — but you can see even more if you want. In your Inbox, pinch and hold an email to preview its contents and see a list of options for replying, filing it, and more.

FIGURE 8-3:
Tap the More
button and
then tap
Remind me to
be reminded
to respond to
an email.

Want to see more than two lines of text for each email (which is the default)? You can choose to see more lines of text without opening the email by opening the Settings app, tapping Apps, tapping Mail, tapping Preview, and then choosing up to five lines!

By default, Mail groups together email messages that are part of the same *conversation* (thread), instead of listing each reply individually. Conversations make it easier to follow a thread and help streamline your Inbox. But you can adjust this setting, if you like. In the Settings app, tap Apps, tap Mail, and then turn on (or off) Organize by Thread. You can also change other settings, such as Collapse Read Messages, Most Recent Message on Top, Show To and Cc labels, and more.

PINNING AN EMAIL IN ANOTHER WINDOW

Did you know you can pinch and hold on a message in your inbox and drag and drop it somewhere else in your field of view? For example, you can see your main Mail app in the center of your view but move a message to the left or right of the "room" you're actually in. It's an efficient use of your space. Simply pinch and move the message and let go where you want it; close it by X-ing out at the bottom or pinch and hold the horizontal bar to move it somewhere else.

Writing and Sending an Email Message

As you would do on your phone, tablet, or computer, you can tap Reply and write back to the sender (or tap Reply to All if there is more than one person in the email correspondence). Here's how to send a message from scratch:

1. **From the Home View, open the Mail app and tap the Compose button in the upper-right corner (it looks like a square with an arrow pointing up out of it).**

   When you hover over the Compose button, you'll see "New Message."

2. **Tap New Message or continue from a Draft message (one you started but haven't sent yet).**

3. **Tap the To field and start typing out the recipient's name (their email address will be automatically added if they're in your Contacts) or type the actual email address from scratch.**

   You can also add more people to the To field if you like, or add someone to the Cc (carbon copy) field or the Bcc (blind carbon copy) field.

   TIP

   After you enter recipients, you can reorder names in the address fields (To, Cc, Bcc), or pinch and drag them from one address field to another — for example, from the Cc field to the Bcc field if you decide you don't want their names to appear to the main recipient.

4. **Tap the Subject field to write what the email is about, and then select the large body of the email (in white) for the main contents of the email.**

5. **Type your message using the virtual keyboard or a compatible Bluetooth keyboard.**

6. **To change the formatting, tap one of the options at the bottom of the email, such as the font style and size, which changes all the text in your message.**

   Alternatively, tap the only the word(s) you want to change, which highlights them, and you can now tweak the font style and color of text, use a bold or italic style, add a bulleted or numbered list, and more.

   TIP

   To automatically send a copy of every email to yourself, in the Settings app, tap Apps, tap Mail, and turn on Always Bcc Myself.

7. **To send an email from a different account (if you have more than one account set up in Apple Vision Pro), tap the Cc/Bcc field, and the From field appears; choose an account you want to send the message from.**

8. **To add an attachment, at the bottom of the message, click the paperclip icon and select a file on your Apple Vision Pro or from a cloud account (like iCloud or OneDrive) and attach it.**

You can also import a photo or short video by clicking the Gallery icon at the bottom of the message, which opens your Gallery on Apple Vision Pro. Select the photo or video you want to attach.

TIP The fastest way to compose an email while wearing Apple Vision Pro? Just use your voice to ask Siri to do it! Regardless of the app you're in, simply say, "Hey Siri, send an email to [name]," and you'll see a pop-up window to compose the message. As long as the person is in your Contacts, it will populate the To field with the recipient's email address, and you can add the subject line and the email itself.

TIP Writing an email on a Saturday or super-late at night and don't want to send it just yet? Pinch and hold the Send button, and then choose when you want to send the email. To see more options, tap Send Later.

TIP If you sent an email and immediately realize you made a mistake, you can unsend the message within 10 seconds. Just open the Sent folder, pinch and hold the message, and tap Undo Send. If you want to have more time to unsend, you can open the Settings app, tap Mail, and change Undo Send Delay from 10 seconds to 20 seconds or 30 seconds. You can also turn this feature off altogether (but I wouldn't!). And, of course, this change will only affect future messages — it won't affect the messages you've already sent.

CHANGING YOUR EMAIL SIGNATURE

An email signature is text that appears at the bottom of every email you send. It might include your job title, phone number, preferred pronouns, or whatever you want.

There are a few good reasons to set up an email signature at the end of your messages. Not only does it look professional to a prospective employer or recruiter, but it conveniently adds info you'd otherwise have to manually type out, such as your phone number or mailing address. This saves you time, because your recipients can just refer to your signature for the info they need. Or, like me, you have all your social media handles at the bottom of every email, which may be a good idea, too!

To add an email signature in Apple Vision Pro, open the Settings app, tap Mail, scroll down to Composing, and select Signatures. By default, the signature is "Sent from my Apple Vision Pro." If you don't like this, delete the text and add something else.

Organizing Your Messages

Email is supposed to make us more productive, but it could have the opposite effect if you're managing a bunch of junk messages, have too many inboxes (from multiple accounts), or don't know which messages take top priority.

You can quickly manage emails with simple gestures, such as moving individual emails to the Trash, marking them as Read, and more.

In this section, I fill you in on tips and tricks to better organize and manage your messages, after you've opened the Mail app.

Managing an individual email

To manage an individual email, open Mail and select a message; then pinch and hold over the message preview (in the middle column, between the Inbox to your left and the contents of the email to the right). The following options appear:

>> Open in New Window

>> Mark (flag the message)

>> Notify Me (set an alarm)

>> Mute message

>> Move Message (to another folder)

>> Archive Message

>> Block Sender

You can also select an email by pinching it and then manually dragging it to another folder on the left of your Mail screen, such as moving something from your Inbox to the Junk or Trash folder. Or moving a message from your Inbox of one account (like Microsoft Exchange) to the inbox on your Gmail.

Managing your mailboxes

You can choose which mailboxes to view, reorder your mailboxes, create new ones, and rename or delete mailboxes.

To manage your mailboxes, tap Edit in the upper-left corner, and then do any of the following:

>> **View mailboxes.** Select the check boxes next to the mailboxes you want to include in the mailboxes list.

>> **Reorder mailboxes.** Pinch and hold the Reorder button next to a mailbox until it lifts up; then drag it to the new position.

>> **Create a new mailbox.** Tap New Mailbox in the lower-right corner, and then follow the instructions.

>> **Rename a mailbox.** Tap the mailbox and then tap the title. Delete the name and then enter a new name.

>> **Delete a mailbox.** Tap the mailbox and then tap Delete Mailbox.

TIP

To move or mark multiple emails, while viewing a list of emails, tap Edit and then select the emails you want to move or mark by tapping their check boxes. To select multiple emails quickly, swipe down through the check boxes. Tap Mark, Move, or Trash at the bottom of the window.

Changing Your Mail Settings

There are literally dozens of settings you can tweak to customize your Mail experience and truly make it your own. Earlier in this chapter, I cover how to be notified when new messages arrive in your inbox and some things to change in the Mail app itself, but most of what you can do is in the Settings app.

Open the Settings app, tap Mail, and you'll see the following settings (and more):

>> Siri & Search

>> Notifications

>> Default Mail App

>> Accounts

>> Preview

>> Show To/Cc Labels

>> Swipe Options

>> Ask Before Deleting

>> Follow Up Suggestions

>> Organize by Thread

» Collapse Read Messages

» Most Recent Message On Top

» Complete Threads

» Blocked Sender Options

» Always Bcc Myself

» Add Link Previews

» Include Attachments with Replies

» Signature

» Undo Send Delay

Searching for an Email in the Mail App

Trying to find that email from your boss where they promised you a raise? In the Mail app on Apple Vision Pro, you can search for emails (see Figure 8-4).

FIGURE 8-4: It's easy to search for an email by keyword, date, or attachments.

Courtesy of Apple, Inc.

Here's how to Search:

1. **Open the Mail app.**

2. **From a mailbox, tap the Search field (it looks like a magnifying glass).**

3. **Type what you're looking for or click the microphone icon inside the Search window to say what you are looking for.**

4. **To make your search more specific, do any of the following:**

   - **Search by timeframe:** After you enter a search word, add a space and enter a timeframe, like "February" or "October 2023."

   - **Where to search:** Tap All Mailboxes or Current Mailbox, just under the search window.

   - **Find all flagged emails:** Type **flag** in the Search field, scroll down, and then tap Flagged Messages.

   - **Find all unread emails:** Type **unread** in the Search field, scroll down, and then tap Unread Messages.

   - **Find all emails with attachments:** Type **attachment** in the Search field, scroll down, and then tap Messages with Attachments.

5. **Select the result you're looking for by looking at the message and pinching your index finger to your thumb.**

3
Having Fun with Apple Vision Pro

Discover how to use Apple Vision Pro to have some fun by yourself or with others online.

Use your Apple Vision Pro to watch movies and TV shows on what appears to be an enormous screen.

Experience "spatial" videos, including interactive content that fully envelops your field of view.

Listen to music, podcasts, and audiobooks while wearing Apple Vision Pro.

Read e-books in Apple Vision Pro and experience its super crisp text, adjustable fonts, and swipe-to-turn functionality.

Get your game on with Apple Vision Pro, including several games and services available at the App Store, including multiplayer titles with video support.

Capture and view incredibly lifelike "spatial" photos and videos that will blow you away.

Chapter **9**

Watching TV and Movies

Apple Vision Pro is an awesome tool for collaborating and communicating, but it's also a perfect device for watching TV and movies, whether it's downloaded content, streaming from services like Apple TV+ or Disney+, accessing mind-blowing Immersive Video (which includes many exclusives to Apple Vision Pro), watching 3D blockbusters, and more.

In this chapter, I cover how to access these amazing video experiences via Apple TV, as well as third-party apps. I also revisit Environments (first introduced in Chapter 4) and explain what you can do with them when it comes to watching video content.

Getting to Know the Apple TV App

Compared to using the Apple TV app on an iPhone, iPad, Mac, or Apple TV, using the app while wearing Apple Vision Pro produces an experience that's second to none. Whether you're reclining on a couch, sitting on an airplane, or lying in bed in a hotel room, watching content in Apple Vision Pro can simulate a huge screen, delivering spatial audio (for added immersion) and even 3D and virtual reality (VR) content to wow you (see Figure 9-1).

FIGURE 9-1:
Watching TV
shows and
movies on the
Apple TV app
inside of Apple
Vision Pro.

In the Apple TV app, you can download or stream your media, organize and view it, and quickly find and continue watching content you may have started watching on another device.

**TECHNICAL
STUFF**

It's easy to be confused by the difference between Apple TV and Apple TV+. Apple TV+ is Apple's streaming video service. The Apple TV app lets you access Apple TV+, as well as your other rented or purchased video content through iTunes (what the program is still called on a PC) or the Apple TV store, special immersive videos for Apple Vision Pro, and more. In other words, Apple TV is the main app, and Apple TV+ is part of it. You don't need to subscribe to Apple TV+ to use the Apple TV app, but your selection of content will be limited if you don't.

REMEMBER

The availability of TV shows and movies through Apple varies based on country or region.

You can open the Apple TV app from the Home View. On the left-hand side of the app is a vertical tab bar. Look at it to highlight various options and jump to:

>> **Search:** Allows you to type in a keyword or two and search for what you're looking for.

>> **Home:** Takes you back to the main home page.

>> **Apple TV+:** Enables you to access content if you subscribe to the service.

>> **MLS Season Pass:** Depending on where you live, you can pay to watch Major League Soccer (MLS) matches.

>> **Sports:** Enables you to find other sports to watch.

>> **Store:** Allows you to preview and buy TV shows and movies.

>> **Library:** Gives you access to everything you've purchased (tied to your Apple ID).

Accessing Content in the Apple TV App

When you launch Apple TV, or if you select the Home button along the vertical tab bar, you'll see a handful of options:

>> **Featured:** Apple content is profiled here, with a video preview in a loop and a description of the content. You can pinch and hold your index finger to your thumb and then swipe left or right to cycle through the recommended content.

>> **Top Chart: Apple TV+:** The top TV shows on Apple TV+. Click the arrow to see everything offered or pinch and drag left or right to see the top TV series.

>> **Free Apple TV+ Premieres:** Even if you don't yet pay for Apple TV+, you can see a lot of content, often the first episode of a series. There are also free trials to take advantage of, as well as promotions, often with companies like wireless phone providers, which may include Apple TV+ for free for a year, so keep your eyes open!

>> **Up Next:** Whether it's your own library of content or Apple TV+ movies you're into, you can see the queued content to play whenever you're ready. To remove an item from Up Next, pinch and hold the item; then tap Remove from Up Next.

TIP

You can also see your Up Next queue in the Apple TV app on your other Apple devices or supported smart TV if you're signed in with your Apple ID. This includes content from other partner networks you subscribe to as well, like MAX, Starz, and others.

>> **Apple Immersive Video Is Here:** Here you can find examples of extraordinary experiences for Apple Vision Pro wearers.

>> **Get Recommendations:** Browse the What to Watch row for editorial recommendations that are personalized for you. Many rows throughout the app feature personalized recommendations based on your channel subscriptions, supported apps, purchases, and viewing interests.

>> **Browse Apple TV Channels:** Scroll down to browse Apple TV+ channels you subscribe to. In the Channels row, browse other available channels; then tap a channel to explore its titles.

>> **Spectacular 3D Movies:** Cycle through a featured collection of movies you can watch in 3D, such as *Avatar: The Way of the Water, Spider-man: Into The Spider-Verse, Dune, Mad Max: Fury Road, Gravity,* and others (see Figure 9-2).

>> **Live Schedule:** See thumbnails and short descriptions of any live content in your country or region, such as a sports match (see Figure 9-3).

>> **Discover Apple Originals:** Find award-winning series, compelling dramas, groundbreaking documentaries, kids' entertainment, comedies, and more — with new items added every month.

FIGURE 9-2:
Watch 3D movies, including *Dune,* on Apple Vision Pro.

Courtesy of Apple, Inc.

You can access a ton of TV shows, movies, and sports inside of Apple Vision Pro, via Apple TV+, as well as realistic 3D movies. Some of it requires a subscription to Apple TV+. Other content can be viewed for free or as a stand-alone rental or purchase.

TIP

If you add your TV provider to Apple Vision Pro, you may be able to watch TV shows and movies from other channels and services included in your TV subscription. Open the Settings app, and tap TV Provider. Then choose your TV provider, if it's offered, and sign in with your provider credentials.

FIGURE 9-3:
Watch live
sports
on Apple
Vision Pro.

Navigating the Apple TV+ content in Apple Vision Pro

Look to the left of the Apple TV app and select Apple TV+ from the vertical tab bar. From there, you can do any of the following:

» Sign up for an account, including a free trial.

» See trending content (TV shows, movies), across all genres.

» Access the Top Chart for Movies. Tap the small arrow beside Movies to open up more options or pinch and swipe left and right to cycle through content.

» See what's up next. In the Up Next on Apple TV+ row, find titles you recently added, play the next episode in a series, or continue watching where you left off.

» See what's new on Apple TV+.

» Browse by category, such as Sci-Fi Films & Series, Kids & Family, Nonfiction Films & Series, Feature Films, Drama Series, and Comedy Series.

» See the entire season of a TV series.

» See descriptions and ratings. Tap an item to read the info you seek.

» See all upcoming content (mostly TV series).

» Depending on the country or region you're in, you may have the option to watch Major League Baseball (MLB) games.

» Search for shows, movies, and more.

This is just a taste of the mains sections to select inside Apple Vision Pro's Apple TV+ offering.

Buy, rent, or preorder media in Apple Vision Pro

There's more to the Apple TV app than just the Apple TV+ service. To buy, rent, or preorder movies and TV shows, look to the left in the Apple TV app and you'll see the vertical tab bar. Select the Store option.

You'll see a ton of content to preview before you buy or rent it. Simply select the show or movie to get details, like a synopsis of the movie or TV series, suggested age rating, review scores, genre, length, and how much it costs to buy or rent.

When you buy a TV show or movie, it's added to your library. If the content you're buying is available to download (it varies), you'll find the downloaded item in your library and you can watch it even when Apple Vision Pro isn't connected to the internet.

REMEMBER

And remember, it's all synchronized between compatible Apple devices, by default, so what you buy or rent on, say, your Apple TV box or a Mac, should also be synced to Apple Vision Pro (unless you've disabled the sync feature on your other device).

When you rent a movie, you have 30 days to start watching it. After you start watching the movie, you can play it as many times as you want for 48 hours, after which the rental period ends. When the rental period ends, the movie is deleted.

When you preorder an item and it becomes available, your payment method is billed and you receive an email notification. If you turned on automatic downloads, the item is automatically downloaded to your Apple Vision Pro.

TIP

If you previously purchased a show or movie in 2D and it's now available in 3D, you can also view it in 3D for free!

Playing rented content in the Apple TV app

The Apple TV app gives you access to your library, which contains shows and movies you've purchased, rented, and downloaded. If you use Family Sharing, you can also view purchases made by family members. All your previously purchased movies and TV shows are available on Apple Vision Pro when you're signed in with the same Apple ID.

To watch a movie you rented, tap Library in the tab bar, tap Rentals, and then tap a movie and do any of the following:

>> **Play the movie.** Tap the Play button to play the movie. The time remaining in the rental period is shown.

>> **Download the movie.** Tap and hold over a movie or show you want to watch and, if it's available, a Download option appears.

>> **Share purchases made by family members.** If you use Family Sharing, you and your family members can share purchases in the Apple TV app. Tap Library, tap Family Sharing, and then choose a family member.

>> **Remove a downloaded item.** Tap Library in the tab bar and then tap Downloaded. Swipe left on the item you want to remove; then tap Delete. Removing an item from your library doesn't delete it from your purchases in iCloud.

REMEMBER

If the TV show, movie, sports, or other content you're watching is too loud, the fastest way to change the volume is to say, "Hey Siri, lower" or "Hey Siri, volume 6" (out of 10). It takes longer and it's not as intuitive, but you can also adjust the volume by looking up to the top of the screen (with your eyes, not your head) and clicking the little down arrow to open Control Center; then drag the volume slider left or right. There is one more way to adjust volume, and it's inside the Cinema Environment (covered later in this chapter).

Watching Apple Immersive Video and 3D Movies

Now this is where things get exciting! Apple Vision Pro owners can also access special content, such as Apple Immersive Videos and 3D movies. Captured by a professional or shot on your Apple Vision Pro (or compatible iPhone, such as the iPhone 15 Pro), Apple Immersive Videos are incredibly lifelike 180-degree up to 8K video recordings, also captured with Spatial Audio, to transform you to another time and place. They put you right inside the action, whether it's in a dense forest or your child's birthday party. It's so real, you'll think you're actually there!

Apple Immersive Videos are a big part of the mind-blowing experience of wearing the headset.

Check out titles like Apple's Wild Life, Alicia Keys: Rehearsal Room, Prehistoric Planet Immersive, and Apple Immersive Adventure — some of which are free.

No doubt you'll feel anxious while watching this woman cross an abyss on a tightrope (see Figure 9-4)!

FIGURE 9-4:
Your jaw will be on the ground while experiencing Apple Immersive Video.

Experiencing Encounter Dinosaurs in Apple Vision Pro

One of the very first things you can do after setting up Apple Vision Pro is trying out the Encounter Dinosaurs experience on Apple Vision Pro, which puts you face-to-face with dinosaurs in this amazing app (see Figure 9-5).

To get started, open the Encounter Dinosaurs app from the Home View, and then tap Start. Now you can:

>> Look at different creatures — they may notice you! Try to touch or interact with them, and they may respond!

>> If you move around during the experience, in the real room you're in, the creatures' eyes will likely follow your movements. (Always stay aware of your surroundings — the experience may limit your ability to see objects around you.)

TIP

Be sure to try the experience multiple times, as your actions can lead to different endings.

FIGURE 9-5:
Live among
dinosaurs and
other creatures
in this
awe-inspiring
interactive
and immersive
experience.

Courtesy of Apple, Inc.

If you want to adjust the settings in Encounter Dinosaurs, tap the Settings button and then adjust one of the following:

>> **Room Dimming:** Allows you to dim your room around the content.

>> **Alignment:** Allows content to automatically adjust to best fit your space.

>> **Audio Descriptions:** For the app to describe what's happening in the experience.

>> **Closed Captions:** Show captions to describe what's happening in the experience.

>> **Interaction Assist:** Lets you choose from a list of actions throughout the experience, instead of moving around your space.

Watch 3D Movies in Apple Vision Pro

You can also buy and rent 3D movies in the Apple TV app! Make a fresh batch of popcorn, launch the 3D flick, and get ready for a wild ride. (Oh, but don't touch your pricy headset with buttery fingers!)

To watch Apple Immersive Video:

1. **Open the Apple TV app.**

2. **Tap Home in the tab bar (on the left).**

3. **Choose any title that says "Apple Immersive."**

Alternatively, navigate to Search and select Only on Vision Pro to access the exclusive content. To see a list of all available Apple Immersive Video titles, search for "immersive." In any app, you can also say, "Hey Siri, show me [Name of the Content]."

To watch 3D movies:

1. **In the Apple TV app, tap 3D movies under Search or Home.**

2. **Select a movie to watch or purchase.**

   You may need to scroll down to the How to Watch section on the show or movie page to buy or rent the 3D version of a movie.

3. **Tap the Play button.**

4. **Tap Play in 3D.**

TIP

You can switch between 2D and 3D at any time. Just tap the Back button to return to the movie details; then tap the Play button to update your selection. If you start a 2D movie on another device that's available in 3D on Apple Vision Pro, you can continue watching it in 3D on Apple Vision Pro (and vice versa).

Again, the Apple TV app gives you access to your library, which contains shows and movies you've purchased, rented, and downloaded. If you use Family Sharing, you can also view purchases made by family members. All your previously purchased movies and TV shows are available on Apple Vision Pro when you're signed in with the same Apple ID.

Watching Movies in an Apple Video Pro Environment

Environments let you transform your physical surroundings into a different place, from White Sands to Yosemite to the Moon. Think of an Environment as expansive wallpaper that can wrap around your view, past your eyesight's periphery, yet the main content you're consuming (like an e-book, email, or website) is in the middle of the screen.

Environments work in the Apple TV app, too. In fact, an Environment is a great way to get lost in a movie. The Environment replaces the room you're in while wearing the headset. In fact, there's an Environment called Cinema that darkens everything around you, so it's as if you're in a pitch-black theater.

If you want to move the TV show or movie around the room you're in and pin it elsewhere (yes, even if you can't see your physical space), look to the bottom of the Apple TV app and stare at the horizontal bar, pinch and hold (by pressing your index finger to your thumb), move the window somewhere else, and let go.

To watch Apple TV in an Environment and hide other windows:

1. **Open Apple TV and start to watch some content.**

2. **While you're watching something, tap the Environments button in the upper-left corner of the window. (It looks like two mountain caps.)**

3. **Choose your current Environment or the Cinema Environment.**

   My recommendation is the Cinema Environment for when you're watching a movie. You won't be distracted by anything else — it's just you and your content.

   Even if you were already in an Environment, other windows are temporarily hidden, and the Apple TV app moves directly into view.

4. **To use a different system Environment, see Use Environments on Apple Vision Pro.**

5. **To see your windows again, tap the Minimize button.**

6. **If you want to adjust your level of immersion, turn the Digital Crown just above your right eye.**

   Twisting the dial left or right will increase or decrease the effect, accordingly.

Remember how I mentioned the Cinema Environment is almost like sitting in a dark movie theater? This is neat: You can choose where you "sit" in the Cinema Environment (which may be called something else in other countries and regions), as if you were at the movies with friends. Look to the bottom of the Cinema Environment, and you'll see "Middle Row." Tap that to change it to the "Front" or "Back." You can also select "Floor" or "Balcony" for height selection.

You can also adjust volume here, skip forward and back between your content, and more.

See Figure 9-6 for what this Cinema Environment looks like and how you can choose where to "sit."

As I cover in Chapter 13, you won't be able to wirelessly cast video to a nearby compatible display (like a Mac or some smart TVs) if there's embedded digital rights management (DRM). That is, TV shows and movies on services like Apple TV+ or Disney+ will appear blacked out during screen sharing via AirPlay.

FIGURE 9-6:
The Cinema
Environment
turns your real
environment
to darkness
and even lets
you select
where you're
viewing the
movie from.

Courtesy of Apple, Inc.

Using Third-Party Streaming Services

As long as there is an Apple Vision Pro app available to use with your favorite streaming services, you can watch content inside the headset to simulate a huge screen.

But there are some caveats and limitations. For example, not all major services (like Netflix or YouTube) are available as of this writing, and even if they are, the virtual screen may not be as big as Apple TV+ content for some reason (but it's still impressive).

Disney+ is one streaming app that's available on Apple Vision Pro, and I'll use that as an example. To get going, follow these steps:

1. **Put on Apple Vision Pro and launch the visionOS App Store from Home View.**

2. **Download the Disney+ app, and sign into your account with your email address and password.**

   Disney+ is not free — it's subscription-based streaming service like Apple TV+ — but it's well worth the cost of admission, in my opinion. If you don't have a membership, sign up for a new account and you get a free trial period in which to test-drive the service.

3. **After choosing your profile, select the Environments icon from the navigation bar to be transported to unique Disney+ viewing environments.**

   There are four to choose from (at the time of this writing):

   - The dusty desert planet Tatooine from *Star Wars*

   - Marvel's Avengers Tower, based on the comic books–turned–blockbuster movies

   - Boo! The zany Scare Floor of *Monsters Inc.* (see Figure 9-7)

   - The opulent Disney+ Theater, inspired by Hollywood's iconic El Capitan Theater

   Environments with a Download icon are all freely available for download.

FIGURE 9-7:
You can select a custom Disney+ Environment inside the Disney+ app.

Courtesy of Apple, Inc.

Disney+ has a ton of 3D content to view, both TV shows and movies. To easily find 3D content, select the 3D Collection icon from the navigation bar.

HEY, WHAT ABOUT NETFLIX?

Netflix isn't available on Apple Vision Pro, but there are two ways to watch Netflix on the device:

- **Web browser:** Open the Safari web browser, go to www.netflix.com, and sign into your account. It's not as immersive as an app, but you can at least choose to watch it full screen, so you don't see it's in a web browser. Netflix is onboard with watching its content in this fashion (see https://help.netflix.com/en/node/134000). Maybe this suggests a dedicated Netflix app for Apple Vision Pro is in the works?

- **Supercut app:** A third-party app called Supercut lets you stream Netflix and other services you may already pay for in up to 4K resolution and with Dolby Atmos sound — and without the letterboxing you'll get when viewing on a web browser.

Chapter **10**

Listening to Music and Podcasts

'm a huge music fan. In fact, before I became a techie, I played drums and managed a rock band. Good times. And though I didn't expect to enjoy hearing music while wearing Apple Vision Pro, the audio quality, huge collection of songs (via Apple Music), and smooth multitasking all helped me appreciate this device for streaming music. And that's exactly what this chapter is about. Well, that and tuning into podcasts, too!

In this chapter, I start with getting music on the device. Then I show you how to find and listen to tracks, manage all this content, and more.

TIP

If you're looking for information on playing audiobooks, turn to Chapter 11.

Exploring the Apple Music App

There are a few ways to enjoy music on Apple Vision Pro. You can stream it from a website or third-party app, but the easiest way is through the Apple Music app, which is already included on Apple Vision Pro — and that includes high-resolution "lossless" audio, too!

Probably familiar to anyone who already owns an Apple device, the Music app is accessible from the Home View screen (or you can say "Hey Siri, open Apple Music"). The app includes access to an (optional and paid) Apple Music subscription, which lets you listen to tens of millions of songs (ad-free). Plus, you can also play music from streaming radio stations or songs you've previously purchased through the Apple Music store or iTunes.

Heck, you can also follow along with the lyrics of songs in Apple Vision Pro (see Figure 10-1).

FIGURE 10-1:
The Apple Music streaming service supports lyrics so you can sing along (and get the lyrics right).

TIP

While you're watching a music video in the Music app, tap the Environments icon (it looks like two mountains) and then select an Environment to view the music video in that Environment.

WARNING

On its website, Apple warns about playing music too loudly and advises you to be aware of your surroundings while using Apple Vision Pro, so you don't risk hurting yourself (or others) around stairs, balconies, railings, glass, mirrors, sharp objects, sources of excessive heat, windows, or other hazards.

Understanding how the Music app is organized

There are a few ways to find and get music to play on Apple Vision Pro:

- ❯❯ **Sign up for Apple Music.** With a subscription and a Wi-Fi connection, stream as much music as you like from the Apple Music catalog and your music library. You can download songs, albums, and playlists, and share music with your friends.

  In other words, unlike paying for downloaded songs one-by-one like you used to with iTunes (for $0.99 per song), Apple Music is more of an all-you-can-eat approach — you pay one lump sum per month and consume as much music as you like. It's important to note you don't own music on Apple Music; you're essentially renting it.

- ❯❯ **Participate in Family Sharing.** Purchase an Apple Music family subscription, and everyone in your Family Sharing group can enjoy Apple Music.

- ❯❯ **Listen to Apple Music radio.** The Music app also gives you access to Apple Music radio, which is three worldwide radio stations — Apple Music 1, Apple Music Hits, and Apple Music Country — broadcasting live on Apple Music. There are also local, national and international stations to listen to.

- ❯❯ **Use the Music MiniPlayer.** Just as you can on your Mac or Windows computer, Apple Vision Pro users can listen to music in the MiniPlayer, which you can have open while you're using other apps. To launch MiniPlayer, look at the album art in the player at the bottom, and then tap the MiniPlayer button.

Note: Services and features aren't available in all countries or regions, and features may vary by region.

REMEMBER

Apple Vision Pro offers surprisingly good audio, but those around you can hear whatever you're listening to. For private listening, you can pair Bluetooth earbuds or headphones. Just open the Settings app and tap Bluetooth.

Playing music

To play music, open the Music app and look to the left, at the vertical tab bar. You'll see the following:

- ❯❯ **Home:** Click to go to the main Home screen inside the Music app. You'll be prompted to sign up for the Apple Music service (with one month free).

- ❯❯ **Radio:** Select one of the streaming radio stations, whether it's one of the three Apple stations or one of the local, national, or international stations listed here, along with the genre.

- ❯❯ **Library:** This is where you can access music you've previously purchased, divided into the following categories:

  - ● Recently Added

- Artists

- Albums

- Songs

- Genres

- Composers

  This includes downloaded songs or those stored online (in the cloud), which require an internet connection.

» **Search:** Click the magnifying glass to look for a particular songs, artist, album, genre, radio station, and more.

To play and control music, you'll notice a player at the bottom of the Music app to show lyrics and play, pause, skip, shuffle, and repeat songs. You can also use Now Playing to view album art, choose what plays next in the queue, and open the MiniPlayer.

Pinch your index finger to your thumb, and select one or more of the following buttons:

» **Play:** Play the current song.

» **Pause:** Pause playback.

» **Next:** Skip to the next song. Pinch and hold to fast-forward through the current song.

» **Previous:** Return to the song's beginning. Tap again to play the previous song in an album or playlist. Pinch and hold to rewind through the current song.

» **More (three dots):** Tap for more options, such as Add to Library or Go to Artist.

» **Lyrics:** Show or hide time-synced lyrics (lyrics not available for all songs). You need an Apple Music subscription to view lyrics.

» **Queue:** See the list of songs that are coming up next.

» **Volume:** Adjust the volume. Tap the Volume button and then pinch and drag the slider.

» **MiniPlayer (see Figure 10-2):** Show the MiniPlayer by looking at the album art in the player at the bottom of the window, and then tap the MiniPlayer button.

Drag to go to a different
part of the song   Close the MiniPlayer

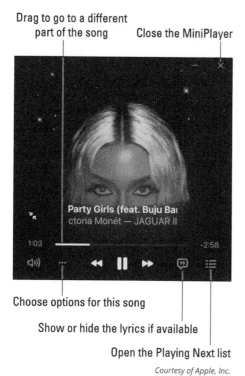

FIGURE 10-2:
The Apple
Music
MiniPlayer
feature helps
you navigate
through
content,
even while
you're inside
another app.

Choose options for this song

Show or hide the lyrics if available

Open the Playing Next list

Courtesy of Apple, Inc.

Subscribing to Apple Music

Similar to other streaming services like Spotify — which is not supported on Apple Vision Pro as of this writing, unless you want to stream from the Spotify website — Apple Music offers tens of millions of ad-free songs, online or off, and a growing number of high-quality tracks with lossless audio and Dolby Atmos technology (which sounds amazing!).

You can subscribe to Apple Music or to Apple One, which is a bundle that includes Apple Music and other services. Qualified students can purchase a student subscription at a discounted price. Not all plans, songs, and features are available in all countries and regions.

If you want to give it a go, subscribe to Apple Music when you first open the Music app. You can also open the Settings app, tap Apps, tap Music, and tap the subscription button.

When you subscribe to Apple Music (or Apple One Family, or Apple One Premier), you can use Family Sharing to share Apple Music with up to five other family members. Your family group doesn't need to do anything — Apple Music is available to them the first time they open the Music app after your subscription begins.

TIP

When a friend or family member shares music with you in Messages, you can easily find it in Shared with You in Apple Music. Music must be turned on in the Settings app (tap Messages and tap Shared with You), and your friend must be in your contacts.

Finding and playing Apple Music content

If you're an Apple Music subscriber, this section is for you! Along with searching for something specifically, it's super fun to browse new and noteworthy music, albums, music videos, playlists, and more.

While wearing Apple Vision Pro, open the Music app and tap Browse to find new music. Then do any of the following:

>> **Explore featured music.** At the top of the page, swipe left and right through featured songs and videos.

>> **Browse playlists created by music experts.** Tap one of the many playlists created by music experts from around the globe.

>> **Explore new music.** Swipe through the newly released albums in this list.

>> **Play music that matches your mood.** As the name suggests, tap a mood, such as Romance or Party, and then tap a relevant playlist.

>> **See what's hot.** What's trending? Tap a song under the Best New Songs heading to find out. Swipe left to see more.

>> **Listen to the top songs from around the world.** Tap one of the Daily Top 100 playlists, in various countries across the world.

>> **Listen to songs from upcoming albums.** Tap an album below Coming Soon and non-grayed-out songs you can hear now.

>> **Browse your favorite categories.** Tap Browse by Category, and then tap a featured playlist, song, album, artist, radio station, or music video.

>> **Play the day's most popular songs.** Tap Charts, and then tap a song, playlist, album, or music video. If you like, tap All Genres at the top of the window to get more specific on the music genre you're into.

>> **Watch music videos.** Tap Music Videos and then tap a featured music video (or playlist of music videos).

Searching for music

The previous section is all about browsing to see what's available, but it's also easy to search for music on Apple Vision Pro. You can quickly browse through music categories, see recent searches, and search Apple Music stored in your library.

Tap Search in the tab bar, and then do any of the following:

>> Tap a category, such as Pop, Rock, Country, Reggae, or Dance.

>> Tap the search field and then tap something you recently chose while searching, such as a specific song, album, or artist.

>> Tap the search field, tap Apple Music or Your Library, and then type something you want to hear.

REMEMBER

Apple Music subscribers can simply summon Siri to ask for a specific song. In anything you're doing in Apple Vision Pro, say, "Hey Siri, play [song, artist, album, music genre] in Apple Music" and it will start. If you don't subscribe to Apple Music, your headset will try to find the song in your library (if purchased) or on Apple Radio.

Adding music to Apple Vision Pro

In the Music app, Apple Music subscribers can add songs and videos from Apple Music to their library. You can stream music you add to Apple Vision Pro when you have an internet connection. But to play music when you're not connected to the internet, you must first download it.

To add music from Apple Music to your library, do any of the following:

>> Pinch and hold a song, album, playlist, or video, and then tap Add to Library.

>> When viewing the contents of an album or playlist, tap the Add button near the top of the window to add the album or playlist, or tap the More button. Then tap Add to Library to add individual songs.

>> In Now Playing (at the bottom of the window), tap the More button and then tap Add to Library.

>> Download a song, album, or playlist by pinching and holding music you've added to your library and then tap Download. After you add a playlist or album, you can also tap the Download button at the top of the window. *Note:* You must turn on Sync Library to download music from Apple Music to your library (open the Settings app, tap Apps, tap Music, and turn on Sync

Library). To always download music, open the Settings app, tap Apps, tap Music, and turn on Automatic Downloads.

If the music you're downloading is available in Dolby Atmos, the Dolby Atmos badge appears next to the item, and you can download it either in Dolby Atmos or in stereo. To download music in Dolby Atmos when available, open the Settings app, tap Apps, tap Music, and turn on Download in Dolby Atmos.

REMEMBER

Remember to select Apple Music's Lossless Audio option for much better sound quality:

1. **Open the Settings app, tap Apps, and tap Music.**

2. **Tap Audio Quality, and tap Lossless Audio to turn it on or off.**

3. **Choose the audio quality for streaming and/or downloading audio.**

To delete music from the library, pinch and hold the song, album, playlist, or music video, and tap Delete from Library.

Music you add to your Apple Vision Pro is also added to other devices if you're signed in to the iTunes Store and App Store using the same Apple ID and you have Sync Library turned on (in the Settings app, tap Apps, tap Music, and turn on Sync Library).

REMEMBER

If you're a fan of Alicia Keys, remember to watch her Alicia Keys: Rehearsal Room Immersive Video (see Chapter 9). In the video, she's jamming in a recording studio with her band and backup singers, and it's like you're *really* there.

Playing Podcasts on Apple Vision Pro

It's easy to stream, subscribe, and play podcasts in Apple Vision Pro. When you hear a podcast you like, you can subscribe to it, so every time there's a new episode, it automatically downloads to your device so you can listen offline when and where you want.

The Podcasts app is an iPad app that works with Apple Vision Pro. As such, you'll find it in the Compatible Apps folder on your Apple Vision Pro's Home View (see Figure 10-3).

FIGURE 10-3:
Tap the
Compatible
Apps folder
from your
Home View to
open Apple
Podcasts.

Compatible Apps

TIP

When you listen to episodes, personalized recommendations appear on the Home page to help you discover your next show. Also, while most podcasts are free, some shows may offer paid subscriptions that give you access to exclusive shows and episodes, new releases, episodes without ads, and more.

To find and browse podcasts, launch the Podcasts app from Home View. (It's in the Compatible Apps folder.) Along the left-hand side, you'll see Home, Browse, Top Charts, Search, and Library (your subscribed-to content). Under Library, you can select Recently Updated, Shows, Channels, Saved, Downloaded, and Latest Episodes.

You can search a podcast by title, person, or topic from the Search tab.

TECHNICAL
STUFF

You can also add shows by website address (URL), by tapping Library, tapping Shows, tapping the More button (three dots), and then tapping Add a Show by URL, which must contain an RSS feed of a podcast.

To play a podcast, tap a podcast and then tap the Play button below the episode title. You can also tap Pause, Rewind (15 seconds), Fast-Forward (30 seconds), Playback Speed (to hear a podcast in 1.5x or 2x, for example, if you're pressed for time).

To change the number of seconds you rewind or skip forward, open the Settings app, tap Apps, tap Podcasts, tap Rewind or Forward, and change the number of seconds.

Are you only interested in the last 10 minutes of a 2-hour podcast? Tap the player at the bottom of the window, and then pinch and drag the slider below the episode's artwork and let go at the desired time.

To resume playing a previous show or episode, tap Home, scroll to the bottom of the window, and then tap an episode below Recently Played.

To set a sleep timer, tap the player at the bottom of the window, and then tap the Sleep Timer. This turns off Apple Podcasts at a certain time (ideal for bedtime).

You can add episodes to Playing Next, to hear it after what you're listening to now, or tap the More button (three dots) below an episode, and then tap Add to Queue to add it to the list of episodes that are playing next (which will play in the order you add them). Want to change the order? In the Queue section, pinch to drag and drop the Reorder button to reorder episodes, if desired, and swipe left to remove an episode, or tap Clear to remove all episodes.

IN THIS CHAPTER

» **Finding and downloading books to read**

» **Reading e-books in Apple Vision Pro**

» **Listening to audiobooks in the headset**

» **Setting reading goals in the Books app**

» **Opening PDFs in Apple Vision Pro**

Chapter **11**

Downloading and Reading E-Books

I know what you're going to say before you even say it: You don't plan on reading books in Apple Vision Pro. But don't write off Apple Vision Pro as an effective way to read a book or flip through a digital magazine! Granted, it's not the lightest device, and you may not want to something over your face, when you can just hold a book, e-reader, or tablet in your hands, but don't knock it 'til you try it!

In this chapter, I cover how to find and download books to your Apple Vision Pro and what the experience is like to read books at home or on the go on the Books app.

But know you can also install other e-readers, too — like Amazon's Kindle or the Barnes & Noble NOOK app — especially if you already have an account (and books) with them. I also cover audiobooks, as well as reading other kind of materials like PDFs, which is how some digital magazines are available.

Downloading Books onto Apple Vision Pro

The Books app (shown in Figure 11-1) is the default book-reading app on Apple Vision Pro.

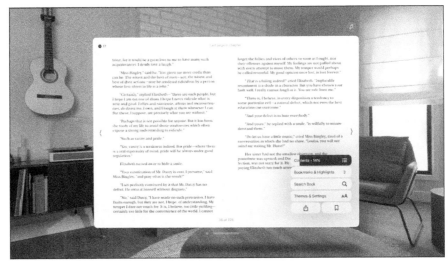

FIGURE 11-1:
The Books
app in Apple
Vision Pro.
Appearance
settings are
visible at the
bottom right.

In fact, Books is an iPad app that works with Apple Vision Pro. It's an e-reader and a bookstore all in one. Text is surprisingly crisp on Apple Vision Pro.

In the Books app, you can find and download today's bestsellers, view top charts, or browse lists curated by Apple Books editors. After you select a book or audiobook, you can almost immediately read or listen to it right in the app. And it will be synchronized with any of your other devices that has the Books app installed, so you can start reading on your Apple Vision Pro and continue on another Apple device, or vice versa.

TIP

To see your books, your progress, and your downloads across your devices where you're signed in with the same Apple ID, open the Settings app, tap your name, tap iCloud, turn on iCloud Drive and Books, and adjust any other settings you want.

From the Home View, look at the Books app, which will be in the Compatible Apps folder, and tap to open it by pressing your index finger to your thumb. Inside, there are three main sections:

>> **Home:** Tap to access the books, audiobooks, and PDFs you're currently reading. You can also get personalized suggestions for your next read, find books you've marked as Want to Read, and daily reading goals, as well as keep track of your finished books.

>> **Library:** Tap All to view all the books, audiobooks, samples, series, and PDFs you've downloaded from the Book Store or manually added to Books. It will look like a virtual bookshelf. If you want, you can see your books sorted into collections, such as Want to Read, Finished, and Downloaded. Library sections include All, Want to Read, Finished, Books, Audiobooks, PDFs, My Samples, and Downloaded.

>> **My Collections:** Organize your books in personalized collections.

Creating a Collection and Adding Books to It

You can create your own collections to personalize your library. Here's how:

1. In the Books app, if you don't see the sidebar icon, which looks like two open book pages, tap the Sidebar button.
2. Tap New Collection.
3. Name the collection whatever you want and tap Done.

To add a book in your library or the Book Store to a collection, tap the More Info button (three dots) below the book cover, tap Add to Collection, and tap the collection. You can add the same book to multiple collections if you want.

To sort books in your library or a collection, follow these steps:

1. In the Books app, if you don't see the sidebar icon, tap the Sidebar button.
2. Tap All or a collection.
3. Tap the More button.
4. Tap Recent, Title, Author, or Manually.

   If you choose Manually, pinch and hold a book cover and then drag it to the position you want.

Tap the Table of Contents button to view books by title or cover.

You can also remove books, audiobooks, and PDFs or hide them on Apple Vision Pro. To do so, follow these steps:

1. **In the Books app, if you don't see the sidebar icon, tap the Sidebar button.**

2. **Tap a section below Library or a collection below My Collections.**

3. **Tap the More button.**

4. **Tap the items you want to remove, and then tap the Trash button and select an option.**

To unhide books and audiobooks that you've hidden, tap Home, tap your account icon, and tap Manage Hidden Purchases.

Buying Books and Audiobooks in the Books App

The Book Store includes sections like "Limited-Time Prices," "Staff Picks," "New & Trending," and "For You" (based on your previous reads).

On the left in the Books app, tap Book Store or Audiobook Store to browse titles, or tap Search to look for a specific title, author, series, or genre. Tap a book cover to see more details, read a sample, listen to a preview, or mark as Want to Read. For every book, you can see the cover, author, publisher, genre, page count, year released, language, customer reviews, book size (measured in megabytes), and more.

Tap Buy to purchase a title or tap Get to download a free title. All purchases are made with the payment method associated with your Apple ID.

If you own books in PDF format, you can download and open them in the Files app or a third-party PDF reader app. There's a PDF section in the Books app, but Apple Vision Pro doesn't let you open downloaded PDFs in the Books app, for some reason; instead, you need to synchronize them from the Books app on another Apple device. But the native Files app works or a third-party PDF reader.

Reading Books on Apple Vision Pro

When you tap a book's cover, it opens to the first page. To turn the page or go back to the previous page, tap the right- or left-page margin or pinch your index finger to your thumb and swipe to the left or right.

If you're returning to a book you've already started, you'll see the last page where you left off.

By default, you'll see two pages at a time, as if you had an open book in your lap. If you want, you can change to one page only by selecting the book icon (with little arrows around it) in the upper-right corner.

To make the virtual pages appear bigger or smaller, look at the lower-right corner of the page; a rounded white curve appears. Pinch your index finger to your thumb and hold it. Then push your arm forward to make the book smaller or pull your arm toward you to make the page bigger.

Click on any page and you'll see a small Menu button appear in the lower-right corner of the page that looks like two horizontal lines and two dots underneath it. Selecting the menu icon lets you see what percentage of the book you've read, search the book, adjust themes and settings (like font size), bookmark, share what you're reading, and more.

To go to a specific page or location, tap the Menu button; tap Search Book; enter a word, phrase, or page number; and tap a result.

To go to a previous reading location, tap the page and then tap the rounded arrow in the upper-left corner of the page. Tap the rounded arrow again, but in the upper-right corner, to go back to your current location.

To use the table of contents, tap the Menu button and then tap Contents.

TIP

To quickly move through a book, pinch and hold Contents; then drag your fingers left or right. Release your fingers to go directly to that location in the book. Fun, no?

To bookmark a page, tap the Menu button and then tap the Bookmark Ribbon. To see all your bookmarks, tap Bookmarks & Highlights, and then tap Bookmarks.

To change the text and page appearance, tap the Menu button, tap Themes & Settings, and then make changes to font and text size, page background color, and more.

To highlight text, add a note, or share a text selection or book link, select a word or phrase to share, and then tap Highlight, Add Note, or Share.

To share your highlights and notes, tap any page, tap the Menu button, tap Bookmarks & Highlights, and then tap Highlights. Tap the highlight or note that you want to share to jump to it, tap it again on the page, and then tap Share.

To close a book, tap the page and then tap the Close button in the upper-right corner. When you finish a book, personalized recommendations will appear to help you discover your next read.

TIP

You can change which side of the window the menu button appears on. Open the Settings app, tap Apps, tap Books, and choose Left or Right below Reading Menu Position.

Listening to Audiobooks on Apple Vision Pro

Want to close your eyes and hear a book read to you? To play an audiobook, do the following:

1. **In the Books app, if you don't see the sidebar icon, tap the Sidebar button.**

2. **Tap Audiobooks and then tap the audiobook cover to play it.**

While the audiobook is playing, use the audio player controls to skip forward or back, adjust the volume and play speed, set a sleep timer, and other options.

If the audiobook contains a supplemental PDF, tap the More button below the audiobook cover in your library, and then tap View Included PDF.

To buy an audiobook, look to the left of the Books app and select Audiobook Store to browse or search, hear samples, and more.

You can also access the popular Audible service via the Safari web browser and play audiobooks in your Apple Vision Pro from there. Maybe there will be an Audible app at some point to make it easier for Audible subscribers, but there isn't one at the time of writing this book.

Setting Reading Goals in the Books App

Apple's Books app isn't just for acquiring and reading books and audiobooks. It can also help you keep track of how many minutes you read every day and how many books and audiobooks you finish each year. This "gamified" approach is a fun way to motivate you to read more.

And just like you can customize your fitness goals, you can personalize your reading goals. By default, your reading goal is set to 5 minutes every day. To change your daily reading goal, follow these steps:

1. In the Books app, if you don't see the sidebar icon, tap the Sidebar button.
2. Tap Home.
3. Scroll down to Reading Goals.
4. Tap Today's Reading.
5. Tap Adjust Goal.
6. Slide the counter up or down to set the minutes per day that you want to read.

When you reach your daily reading goal, you receive a notification from Books. Tap the notification to get more details about your achievement or send your achievement to friends.

Don't see these notifications? Make sure your Books notifications are turned on by opening the Settings app, tapping Notifications, tapping Books, and then turning on Allow Notifications. To count PDFs toward your reading goal, open the Settings app, tap Apps, tap Books, and turn on Include PDFs. (This setting isn't on by default.)

To change your yearly reading goal (set to three books per year, by default), follow these steps:

1. In the Books app, if you don't see the sidebar icon, tap the Sidebar button.
2. Tap Home.
3. Scroll down to Books Read This Year.
4. Tap a placeholder square or a book cover.
5. Tap Adjust Goal.
6. Slide the counter up or down to set the number of books you want to read per year.

When you reach your yearly reading goal, you receive a notification from Books. Tap the notification to get more details about your achievement or send your achievement to friends.

To see your reading streaks and records, tap Home and then swipe down to Reading Goals.

You can turn on coaching to receive encouragement and nudges to help you reach your reading goals. Tap your account icon in the upper-right corner, tap Notifications, and turn on Coaching.

To turn off reading goals notifications, tap Home, tap your account icon in the upper-right corner, tap Notifications, and turn off Goal Completion. To clear your reading data, such as time spent reading and reading streaks, open the Settings app, tap Apps, tap Books, and tap Clear Reading Goals Data.

Don't like reading goals at all? Turn off reading goals by opening the Settings app, tapping Apps, and tapping Books.

Reading PDFs

The Books app on Apple Vision Pro supports PDFs documents, too. In fact, the app lets you open and save PDFs that you receive in Mail, Messages, and other apps.

To open a PDF you receive in the Books app, tap the PDF attachment to open it, tap the Share button, and then tap Books. That's it!

To share or print a PDF, open the PDF, tap the Share button, and then choose a share option (such as AirDrop, Mail, or Messages) or tap Print.

To mark up a PDF, open the PDF and tap the Markup button to use the drawing and annotation tools. (Tap near the center of a page if you don't see the Markup button.)

TIP

Apple lets you open and read PDFs in the Files app, but there are also more robust third-party apps for Apple Vision Pro, like Readdle's PDF Expert, shown in Figure 11-2.

FIGURE 11-2:
Readdle's PDF
Expert gives
you more
functionality
for reading
PDFs than
you can find
in Apple's
Books app.

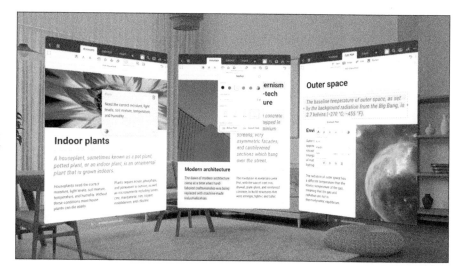

Courtesy of Readdle

Chapter **12**
Playing Games

"Shall we play a game?" This is what the creepy AI asked Matthew Broderick's computer-loving character in the 1983 movie *WarGames*. Fast-forward to today and gaming has matured quite a bit from the text-based war game in that '80s flick. Look no further than the wearable Apple Vision Pro, which dishes up a ton of great gaming experiences.

In this chapter, I explain how to download and launch games in Apple Vision Pro. I explain immersive spatial games are — including What the Golf?, Super Fruit Ninja, and Game Room, a collection of classic card games and board games. Finally, I also explain how to play multiplayer games with spatial Personas (see Chapter 2) and casual games during a FaceTime call.

Finding and Downloading Games onto Apple Vision Pro

The App Store offers excellent games you can play while wearing the headset. Some are tied to the Apple Arcade subscription service, including new spatial games that magically transform the space around you to put you in the middle of the action. You can also play compatible iPad and iPhone games on your virtual big screen.

To find games to play on Apple Vision Pro, follow these steps:

1. **From the Home View, look at and then open the App Store by pressing your index finger to your thumb.**

2. **In the App Store, look to the left of the screen to see the vertical tab bar.**

3. **Choose Apps & Games (which is what you'll see by default), Arcade (to access games as part of the optional Apple Arcade service), and Search (to enter a keyword).**

When you're browsing in the Apps & Games area of the App Store, you'll see various sections like What We're Playing, New Games for Apple Vision Pro, iPad and iPhone Games for Vision Pro, and What Are You in the Mood For? And shown in Figure 12-1, featured games and apps rotate in a carousel when you land at the App Store; you can swipe across and find something that looks good to you. Half the fun is exploring for yourself to see the charts and curated collections!

To scroll through the App Store, simply press your index finger to your thumb and hold before swiping up or down.

To download a game for Apple Vision Pro, follow these steps:

1. **Select a game.**

   You can read a short description, see screenshots or videos of the game, see a recommended age rating, see what genre the game is (for example, action or puzzle), see who the developer is, see how big the game is (measured in megabytes or gigabytes), and more.

2. **To download the game, click Get (which means the game is free) or the price (which means you have to pay for it).**

   If you have to pay for the game, the credit card you have associated with your Apple account will be charged.

   You're prompted to double-click the top button (over your left eye) to install the game. Optic ID launches to verify you're the one buying the game before processing the payment (this is also required when the game is free).

   When the game is downloading, you'll see the Get or price icon begin to spin and fill in, which tells you how much of the game has installed. The bigger the game (or the slower your internet speed), the longer the dial will take to fill in.

When you open the game for the first time, you may see a question from Apple that says "Allow [game] to track your activity across other companies' apps and websites? The information will be used to reduce the number of relevant ads." You can tap Allow or Ask App Not to Track (my recommendation).

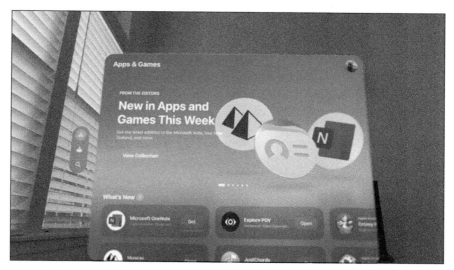

FIGURE 12-1:
Launch the
App Store
inside of Apple
Vision Pro,
and you'll see
a handful of
supported
games.

Courtesy of Apple, Inc.

When the game is open, you can look at the bottom of the game and grab the white horizontal bar (by pinching your index finger to your thumb and holding it) and then move the screen to another part of your room. Or you can look at the white dot at the bottom of the game, which will turn into an X; then you can tap the X to close the game.

TIP

Because Apple Vision Pro has the Safari browser, you can essentially play any browser-based PC games. Or better yet, if you're a fan of Steam, a digital store with thousands of games, you can install the Steam Link app on Apple Vision Pro and play all your PC games via Steam. So, yes, you can play Resident Evil 4 on what appears to be a huge TV, with the Moon environment around you to complete the effect!

Playing Games in Apple Vision Pro

There are two main kinds of games to play in Apple Vision Pro:

>> Select iPhone or iPad games that work inside the headset, which makes it look like you're playing on a huge TV or monitor

>> Spatial games that take advantage of Apple Vision Pro's mixed reality technology

Unless you use a controller (see the next section), all games will be controlled using your hands in the air — just like all other aspects of Apple Vision Pro. In Solitaire, for example, you can look at a card and tap it (pressing your index finger to your thumb), which moves the card into the right space. In another game, you may pinch and hold to grab a card, move it somewhere else on the board, and let go to place it there.

TIP

Some games may require a little trial and error to master the controls. Be sure to go into the Settings area of any game to see if there are any guides, tips, or ways to tweak the controls to make it easier to play.

Spatial games combine the digital/virtual elements of the game — like LEGO pieces or flying fruit — and let you play in your real-world environment, because you can see through the visor. For example, you may see wooden Jenga-like pieces on the real table in front of you, but the tower of game pieces is not there in real life, of course.

Some spatial games encourage exercise, which is a fun way to work out. You may be punching and kicking virtual objects as they approach you in a combative rhythm game.

At the time of this writing, most of the spatial games are playable on Apple Arcade, the popular subscription service that works on multiple Apple devices (iPhone, iPad, Apple TV, Mac, and Apple Vision Pro), and includes more than 250 ad-free games (without the option to buy more content for real money). In the United States, Apple Arcade costs $6.99 per month (at the time of writing). See Figure 12-2 for a look at some of the spatial titles.

Here are a handful of available spatial games playable via Apple Arcade:

>> **Alto's Odyssey — Remastered:** A relaxing "sandboarding" adventure

>> **Bloons TD 6+:** An award-winning tower defense game

>> **Crossy Road Castle:** An arcade game built for cooperative fun

>> **Cut the Rope 3:** A puzzle game that includes real-world physics

>> **Game Room:** Classic games like Klondike Solitaire, Checkers, Chess, Sea Battle (Battleship), and more

>> **Gibbon: Beyond the Trees:** An arcade game with an ecological message

>> **Illustrated:** Jigsaw puzzles with stories

>> **Jetpack Joyride 2:** A classic iPhone game with the Apple Vision Pro treatment

FIGURE 12-2:
Apple Arcade
on Apple Vision
Pro includes
many spatial
games.

>> **LEGO Builder's Journey:** A game in which you built your own worlds using LEGO pieces

>> **Patterned:** A unique puzzle game featuring seamless, repeating patterns

- >> **Solitaire Stories:** A handful of Klondike and Spider Card Games

- >> **Spire Blast:** A physics-based match puzzler

- >> **stitch.:** A puzzle game with beautiful graphics

- >> **Super Fruit Ninja (see Figure 12-3):** A game in which you slice and dice fruit with your hands

- >> **Synth Riders:** A mesmerizing music game

- >> **What the Golf?:** A funny take on the popular sport

- >> **Wylde Flowers:** A magical life simulation

Game availability varies based on country and region.

REMEMBER

Using a Bluetooth Game Controller

Most games you download and play on Apple Vision Pro work with your hands, but some just work better with a wireless controller. Fret not! Apple Vision Pro supports Bluetooth accessories, including game controllers.

To pair the controller, open the Settings app, tap Bluetooth, and search for nearby devices. You may need to press a little button on the controller to make it visible (check the instruction manual for the Bluetooth game controller if you need help).

After you pair a compatible game controller, you can customize it for supported games from Apple Arcade and the App Store, by opening the Settings app, tapping General, and tapping Game Controller. Choose an option for buttons you want to change, or tap Add App to create custom controls for a certain app.

To unpair a Bluetooth device, open the Settings app, tap Bluetooth, tap the Information button next to the name of the device, and tap Forget This Device. Don't see your controller in the Devices list? Make sure Bluetooth is turned on in Apple Vision Pro.

To quickly disconnect from all Bluetooth devices without turning Bluetooth off, open Control Center and tap the Bluetooth button.

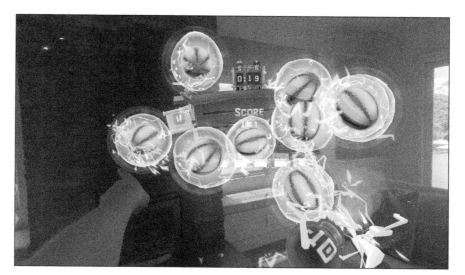

FIGURE 12-3:
Fruit was never
this exciting!
In Super Fruit
Ninja for Apple
Vision Pro, use
your hands
to slice and
dice through
fruit in order
to rack up as
many points as
possible.

Courtesy of Apple, Inc.

SharePlaying Games Using Spatial Personas

Your spatial Persona (see Chapter 6 for more info) is available in some games, like Game Room in Apple Arcade, which is controlled by your eyes, hands, and voice. Game Room is a collection of spatial board and card games that are playable in Apple Vision Pro. Some of the games are:

>> **Chess:** The classic two-player game of wits

>> **Solitaire:** A solo card game

>> **Hearts:** The beloved card game tied to collecting suits

>> **Yacht:** A take on Yahtzee, where you roll the dice and rack up the points

>> **Sea Battle:** A version of Battleship, where you're tasked with sinking enemy ships before they sink yours

REMEMBER

The spatial Persona feature is still in beta at the time of this writing. By the time you're reading this book, it may be an official feature.

Playing with Friends in Game Center

Earlier in this chapter, I mention that there are two main ways to play games in Apple Vision Pro:

>> Select iPhone or iPad games that work inside the headset

>> Spatial games that take advantage of Apple Vision Pro's mixed reality technology

There is a third way, and it's also available on most other Apple devices. I'm referring to Game Center, which lets you send friend requests, manage your public profile (for other games to see), earn achievements, compete on leaderboards, and play games during a FaceTime call.

To get started, set up your Game Center profile by opening the Settings app, tapping Game Center, turning on Game Center, and signing in with your Apple ID. Then do any of the following:

>> **Choose a nickname.** Tap Nickname and enter a name or choose one of the suggestions. Your friends see your nickname when you play games together.

>> **Personalize your avatar.** Tap Edit Avatar and either use an emoji or customize how your initials appear.

>> **Add friends.** In the Settings app, tap Game Center, tap your profile, tap Friends, tap Add Friends, and enter their phone number or Apple ID, or tap the Add Contact button to invite someone in your Contacts list. Recipients can respond to friend requests in Messages (tap the link), inside a supported game (tap the Game Center profile picture, tap Friends, and then tap Friend Requests), or in the App Store itself by tapping the My Account button or your picture at the top right, then tapping Game Center, and finally, selecting Friend Requests.

In your list of friends, tap a friend to see the games they recently played and their achievements.

To play games with friends using SharePlay:

>> Find and download a Game Center multiplayer game in the App Store and play with friends while on a FaceTime call.

>> During a FaceTime call, open a supported multiplayer game, tap Start SharePlay, and follow the instructions.

Here are some of the SharePlay-supported games you can play in a FaceTime call:

» **Heads Up!:** Made famous by Ellen DeGeneres, other players give you hints for you to guess the word hovering above your head that you can't see. For example, if you need to guess the word *alligator,* the other players may say "Long green reptile with sharp teeth" or "Very similar animal to a crocodile."

» **SharePlay Guessing Game:** Guess the phrase or guess the drawing (like Pictionary).

» **Shhh!:** Guess who is the spy.

» **Kahoot!:** Play and create quizzes.

» **Piano with Friends:** Tap the virtual keys while on a FaceTime call.

Chapter **13**

Capturing Photos and Videos

June 2023 was the first time I tried on Apple Vision Pro, at Apple's headquarters in Cupertino, California. It was a guided 30-minute demo, where I got to wear this magical device and try out the gestures, see some immersive videos, and engage in my first FaceTime call with Personas (see Chapter 2).

But what really blew me away were the spatial videos in Apple Vision Pro, where you're playing back a previously recorded scene (in this case, it was a home movie of kids blowing candles on a birthday cake), and it truly felt like I was there at that exact moment because it was in 3D. I was getting goosebumps from someone else's memory — and I immediately envisioned what it would be like to see my *own* kids in this headset. Or what about when my parents are gone, and I can slip on a headset and seemingly be in front of them again?

In this chapter, I explain how to shoot and play back spatial images, as well as how to view and share regular photos and videos in Apple Vision Pro. I also cover how to take screenshots inside of Apple Vision Pro and shoot videos from your perspective, as well as how to share or cast the visual content to a nearby screen for others to see.

Checking Out the Photos App

On the main Home View screen, you see the Photo app (see Figure 13-1). Look at the app, and then tap your index finger to your thumb to open it.

FIGURE 13-1:
The Photos
app on the
main Home
View screen.

Courtesy of Apple, Inc.

After you open the app, you can find and view all the photos and videos on your Apple Vision Pro, which are tied to your Apple ID (so the images you've captured on iPhone and iPad are synchronized via iCloud and viewable here, if you've set up iCloud syncing). Using the tab bar on the left, you can easily browse your photos, divided into the following categories:

>> **Spatial:** This is where you can see all your spatial photos and videos.

>> **Memories:** View your memories in a personalized feed.

>> **Library:** Browse your photos and videos organized by day, month, years, and all photos. The Years, Months, and Days views are curated by Apple to show your best shots.

>> **Albums:** View albums you created or shared.

>> **Panoramas:** See your horizontal panoramas curated.

>> **Search:** Instead of browsing, this is where you can search for photos by location, contents, and more.

When you view photos and videos on Apple Vision Pro, your view is automatically dimmed. To turn off automatic dimming, tap the More button (three dots) while viewing a photo and then tap Auto Dimming.

Figure 13-2 offers a look at how photos and videos are organized in Apple Vision Pro. If you're signed into the same Apple ID as other devices, you'll see those photos and videos here, too.

FIGURE 13-2: Similar to other Apple devices, photos and videos are organized into categories on the Photos app.

Courtesy of Apple, Inc.

Viewing Photos and Playing Videos

To view a photo in the Photos app, simply look at it and then tap to open it. When the photo is dominating much of your view, pinch with both hands and drag apart to zoom in on the photo. Alternatively, move your hands back together to zoom out.

A Live Photo is when your device records what happens 1.5 seconds before and after you take a picture. If you have Live Photos to view, you can pinch and hold a photo with the Live Photo button to see it move like a short video clip.

Tap a video to play it. You can use the player controls to pause, mute, or unmute.

To view a panoramic photo (like the one in Figure 13-3), tap Panorama in the tab bar, and then tap the photo. To immerse yourself in the photo, tap the Immersive button in the upper-right corner.

FIGURE 13-3:
Wow, that's wide! You can truly appreciate panoramic photos inside Apple Vision Pro.

Taking a Screenshot or Video with Apple Vision Pro

Taking a screenshot or video of your view while wearing Apple Vision Pro is super simple. And after you do, you can easily share those images with friends, family, or colleagues, if you want.

When you capture what's in your view while wearing Apple Vision Pro, the photo or video you capture will include everything you see at that moment — the app you're in (or Home View or Settings), the physical room you're in, and the Environment (the wraparound wallpaper; see Chapter 4).

All screen recordings (photos and videos) are saved to the Photos app.

As a clever privacy feature, the photo or video of what you see in Apple Vision Pro may be captured and shared, but it's obscured while you enter a password or passcode.

Taking a screenshot

To capture a screenshot of your view, do one of the following:

» Simultaneously press the Digital Crown (over your right eye) and the top button (over your left eye).

» Say, "Siri, take a screenshot."

You'll hear a camera shutter sound effect, and the screenshot will automatically be saved to the Photos app.

Recording a video

To capture a video of your view, you'll need to first open Control Center (see Chapter 5) by looking up with your eyes (*not* tilting your head) while wearing Apple Vision Pro and tapping the Control Center button when it pops up (it looks like a little downward-facing arrow).

In the Control Center, tap the expanded Control Center tab (which looks like two oval buttons or switches that can be toggled), and then press the Recording button to start the recording. To stop recording, tap the Recording button again, or tap the red status bar at the top of your view and then tap Stop. The recording is saved to the Photos app.

TIP

If you don't see the Recording icon in the Control Center, open the Settings app and tap Control Center to add it.

Sharing your screenshot or video

All captured screenshots and videos are saved to your Photos app on Apple Vision Pro, so the Photos app is where you'll go to view them and share them. Just follow these steps:

1. **From Home View, open the Photos app.**
2. **Select Albums (on the left-hand side).**
3. **Select the screenshot(s) or video(s) you want to share.**
4. **Tap the three horizontal dots in the upper right of the screen.**
5. **Tap Share.**

6. **Tap the method you want to use to share it.**

   Your options include Messages, Mail, AirDrop, and more.

7. **Select who you want to send it to.**

TIP

If you're logged into another Apple device, such as an iPhone, with the same Apple ID, you'll see the screenshots and videos you captured on that device, too, because iCloud synchronizes all photos and videos by default. If you find it easier to share the screenshots and videos you've captured on Apple Vision Pro from another device, you can do that.

Capturing, Viewing, and Sharing Spatial Photos and Videos

Spatial photos and videos look like they're 3D when played back inside Apple Vision Pro (see Figure 13-4). You may not want to wear a headset to capture a memory, but you won't regret it later when you play back the fully immersive images.

FIGURE 13-4:
Choose a spatial photo or video and then tap the Immersive button to really feel like you're there.

Courtesy of Apple, Inc.

TIP
If you take spatial videos on iPhone 15 Pro or iPhone 15 Pro Max (see the nearby sidebar), you can share them with people who own Apple Vision Pro to view on their device. (They'll appear in 2D on other devices.) In June 2024, Apple announced a partnership with Canon, which is developing the RF–S7.8mm F4 STM DUAL lens for its popular Canon EOS R7 camera, so you can record spatial videos with the lens and relive those memories on Apple Vision Pro.

To take a spatial photo or video with Apple Vision Pro, follow these steps:

1. **Press the top button to open Capture.**

2. **Choose whether you want to take a spatial photo or video by tapping Photo or Video at the bottom.**

3. **Press the top button to take a spatial photo or start recording a spatial video.**

4. **To stop recording, press the top button again, or tap the Stop Recording button.**

All images or videos are saved to the Photos app.

TIP
Apple offers these "best practices" for capturing spatial photos and video:

>> **Try to keep your head still while recording spatial video.** A crosshair appears in the center of your view while recording spatial video. If you move too much, the crosshair appears to move outside a circle. Try to keep the crosshair inside the circle for the most comfortable viewing experience.

>> **Before you start a recording, a level appears through the shutter button if you tilt your head.** You can use this level as a guide to help make your photos and videos, well, more level.

>> **Avoid capturing photo or video with subjects that are very close to you physically.**

To view the spatial photo or video you just captured, tap the thumbnail image in the lower-left corner.

To share a spatial capture, follow these steps:

1. **Open the Photos app.**

2. **Find the spatial photo or video you want to share.**

3. **Tap the More button (three dots).**

4. **Tap the Share button.**

5. Select an option such as AirDrop, Mail, or Messages.

6. Select a recipient or type in their info manually (if they aren't in your Contacts).

You can share any photo or video you see inside of Apple Vision Pro by selecting it, tapping the Share icon (which looks like a box with an arrow sticking up from it), and then selecting how you want to send it, such as in a message (Chapter 7), email (Chapter 8), and so on.

You can also attach images to a message or email by clicking the paperclip attachment and then selecting a photo or video.

To view spatial photos and videos, tap Spatial in the tab bar to the left side of the Photos app, and then choose a spatial photo or video. To immerse yourself in the photo, tap the Immersive button. If the video contains excess motion, an alert appears to let you know that watching the video could cause discomfort.

CAPTURING SPATIAL IMAGES USING AN IPHONE

You probably don't want to be wearing a big headset when your kids are singing "Happy Birthday" or when you're in a place that's not conductive for Apple Vision Pro, like behind a waterfall. Fortunately, spatial video recording is available on iPhone 15 Pro and iPhone 15 Pro Max models (running iOS 17.2 or later) and newer iPhones, too. You can play back those 3D images inside of Apple Vision Pro.

To record spatial video on your iPhone, follow these steps:

1. Open the Camera app on your compatible iPhone.

2. Select Video mode.

3. Rotate your iPhone to landscape orientation.

4. Tap the Spatial Video Off button.

5. Tap the Record button or press either volume button to start recording.

6. Tap the Record button or press either volume button again to stop recording.

7. Tap the Spatial Video On button to turn off spatial video recording.

For best results, Apple suggests the following as you record:

- Keep your iPhone steady and level. A tripod or selfie stick can help stabilize the image, too.

- Frame your subjects 3 to 8 feet from the camera.

- Use lighting that is even and bright.

After you record a spatial video, you can view it in 3D in the Photos app on your Apple Vision Pro or view it in 2D on any other device.

Spatial videos captured on iPhone 15 Pro and iPhone 15 Pro Max are recorded at 1080p at 30 frames per second (fps) in standard dynamic range (SDR). One minute of spatial video is approximately 130MB, which is about twice as big as one minute of regular 1080p 30 fps video (at approximately 65MB).

Note: Because spatial videos are synchronized to all your Apple devices (where you're signed in with the same Apple ID and have iCloud Photos turned on), those spatial videos captured on iPhone 15 Pro or iPhone 15 Pro Max (or newer) will be ready to view on Apple Vision Pro. Apple has announced that third-party apps will be able to record spatial photos and videos in the iOS 18 operating system.

Looking at Memories

The Memories feature in the Photos app (see Figure 13-5), available on any Apple device, creates a personalized collection of photos and videos that are set to music, which you can watch like a sentimental slideshow. Each memory features a significant person, place, or event from your Photos library.

To play a memory while wearing Apple Vision Pro, follow these steps:

1. **Open the Photos app.**

2. **Tap Memories in the tab bar off to the left.**

3. **Tap a memory to play it.**

    As you watch, you can do any of the following:

    - Tap anywhere in the app window to see the playback controls (if they're not visible).

    - Tap the Pause button.

    - Swipe left or right, or pinch and drag the frames at the bottom of the window, to go backward or forward.

FIGURE 13-5:
Apple creates Memories based on your photos, and ties them together into a slideshow set to music, which you can view and share with others.

To share a memory, tap Memories in the tab bar, and then play the memory you want to share. While the memory plays, tap the window, tap the Share button, and choose how you want to share.

To add a memory to Favorites, tap the window while a memory is playing, tap the More button, and then tap Add to Favorites. To view your favorite memories, tap Memories in the tab bar, and then tap Favorites at the bottom of the window.

To edit the title and length of a memory, tap the More button in the upper-right corner of the memory, and then tap an option, like Edit Title, Short, Medium, or Long.

To delete a memory, tap the More button in the upper-right corner of the memory you want to delete, and then tap Delete Memory.

According to Apple, sometime in 2024 the visionOS 2 operating system update will allow you to turn a regular 2D photo into a spatial one to view inside of Apple Vision Pro.

Casting Content from Apple Vision Pro to Another Screen

Whether it's viewing photos or maps, playing games or collaborating on a business document, you can share your view of Apple Vision Pro so others around you can see what you're seeing and doing inside the headset.

In fact, it's super easy to mirror your view onto another screen, such as a Mac, Apple TV (connected to a TV or monitor), iPhone, iPad, or compatible smart TV. This is done through AirPlay, which is a popular (and exclusive) Apple feature that lets more than one device in the same area share content (like easily sending photos from your iPad to a friend's iPhone). As shown in Figure 13-6, you can look at, say, a map in Apple Vision Pro, but share it to another screen for others to see what you see.

FIGURE 13-6:
Using Apple's proprietary AirPlay feature, you can wirelessly cast your content to another screen, such as a Mac.

Courtesy of Apple, Inc.

To take advantage of this feature, open Control Center by looking up inside Apple Vision Pro and tapping the Control Center button. Then follow these steps:

1. **Open Control Center and then tap the expanded Control Center button, which looks like two oval switches with dots in them.**

2. **Tap the Options button.**

3. **Tap the Mirror My View button, which looks like two overlapping screens.**

4. **Choose a compatible device from the list of available devices.**

   Only devices that are connected to the same Wi-Fi network as your Apple Vision Pro will appear in this list.

TECHNICAL
STUFF

   A compatible smart TV will need to support AirPlay in order for you to wirelessly share your Apple Vision Pro content to it. Refer to the TV's instruction manual to see if it supports AirPlay. To set it up to receive content, which may only be required once, open the TV's Settings area to see how to activate AirPlay. Many TVs today, from brands like LG, Samsung, and Sony, support AirPlay.

If you don't see your device listed, make sure the device is logged onto the same Wi-Fi network as the Apple Vision Pro. If the two devices are on the same Wi-Fi network and you still don't see your device listed, you may need to manually turn on AirPlay (or AirPlay Receiver) on the other device. Here's how:

- **iPhone or iPad:** In the Settings app, tap General, tap AirPlay & Handoff, and turn on AirPlay Receiver. You can also adjust who can AirPlay to your device or set a passcode.

- **Mac:** In the System Settings app, tap General, tap AirDrop & Handoff, and turn on AirPlay Receiver. (If you're on a Mac running macOS 12 or earlier, open System Preferences, tap Sharing, and then turn on AirPlay Receiver.) You can also adjust who can AirPlay to your device or set a passcode.

- **Apple TV:** Open the Settings app, select AirPlay and HomeKit, and select AirPlay to turn it on.

REMEMBER

Your view on Apple Vision Pro is shared on the screen you selected, like a nearby Mac, but no one can see when you enter a password or passcode, which is a great privacy feature.

TIP

If you don't want people to see your personal notifications come through on your Apple Vision Pro, you can choose to hide notifications when you're sharing your view. In the Settings app, tap Notifications, tap Screen Sharing, and turn Allow Notifications off.

TECHNICAL
STUFF

Depending on what you're sharing, your Apple Vision Pro may not look as great on the external display as it does on the twin 4K screens in front of your eyes. The headset can be shared to the outside display at only up to 720p HD (not 1080p HD or 4K).

WARNING

You can't share videos with digital rights management (DRM) embedded in them. TV shows and movies on services like Apple TV+ or Disney+ (see Chapter 9) will appear blacked out during screen sharing via AirPlay.

Although they are similar, wirelessly sharing your Apple Vision Pro to a nearby screen for others to see isn't the same thing as using your Mac as an extension of Apple Vision Pro, which is more of a productivity tool (see Chapter 16).

4

Being Productive with Apple Vision Pro

Explore the different ways to access online content in Apple Vision Pro, including the integrated Safari web browser (and what makes it unique in the headset).

Find out how to remain productive in Apple Vision Pro, such as mastering the Freeform app for collaborative projects with colleagues, taking advantage of the Notes app, and mirroring your content to a nearby Mac.

Chapter **14**

Searching the Web with Safari

Browsing the web is super-easy (and smooth) while wearing Apple Vision Pro. Apple's own web browser, called Safari, lets you browse and search the web. At the time of this writing, a few third-party web browsers were also available for download and use at the App Store, but none of the big names, like Google Chrome. (That will likely change in the coming months, so if you're a devoted Chrome user, be sure to check the App Store!)

In this chapter, I explain how to browse the web, conveniently preview web links inside Apple Vision Pro, translate web pages, save content to read later, download files, and more.

TIP

If you sign in to iCloud with the same Apple ID on all your devices, you can see all the web pages you have open in Safari on your other devices. You can also keep your bookmarks, history, and Reading List up to date on all your devices.

Browsing and Searching the Web in Apple Vision Pro

From the main Home View screen, look at the Safari app and tap your index finger to your thumb to open it. Figure 14-1 shows what the Safari browsing experience looks like in Apple Vision Pro.

FIGURE 14-1:
Kick back and relax to browse the web, clearly and comfortably, while wearing Apple Vision Pro.

Just as you would in another web browser, you can type a web address (like www.dummies.com) in the Smart Search field at the top of the screen. You can also visit a search engine (like Bing, DuckDuckGo, Google, or Yahoo!) to search the web. You can also just type keywords in the Smart Search field to try to find what you're looking for — if you do that, Safari will use the default search engine to search the web.

TIP

To change your default search engine, open the Settings app, tap Apps, tap Safari, and tap Search Engine.

To search for specific information on a website, enter the name of a website followed by a search term in the Smart Search field. For example, enter **Rotten Tomatoes Dune 2** to search the Rotten Tomatoes review website for the film *Dune: Part Two*. (To turn this feature on or off, open the Settings app, tap Apps, tap Safari, and tap Quick Website Search to turn the option On or Off.)

If you prefer to talk rather than type, look at the Dictation button in the Smart Search field to dictate your search. Or from anywhere in Apple Vision Pro, say, "Siri, visit Rotten Tomatoes in Safari."

When you get results, tap a search suggestion or tap Go on the keyboard.

You can also tap Favorites to see your favorites as suggestions.

Previewing Websites in Safari

Conveniently, the Safari app on Apple Vision Pro has an easy way to preview a website without opening the link. If you see a web address, simply look at it to highlight it; then pinch your index finger to your thumb and hold them together. Safari shows you a preview of the site without your having to open it, as shown in Figure 14-2.

FIGURE 14-2:
You can preview websites before you open them in Safari by pinching and holding over the link.

Courtesy of Apple, Inc.

To open the link, tap the preview, or tap Open in New Tab or Open in Background.

To close the preview and stay on the current page, tap anywhere outside the preview.

Viewing, Saving, and Sharing Websites in Safari

You can easily browse the web on Apple Vision Pro in Safari just as you're used to doing on other devices, like your phone or laptop. Basic stuff. But here are a few other things you can do:

>> **Open multiple Safari windows.** Pinch and drag a link or tab into an empty space in your view.

>> **Refresh the page.** Pinch and drag down from the top of the page or tap the Refresh button on the right side of the Smart Search field.

>> **Share, bookmark, mark up, or add a web page to your Reading List or Favorites.** Tap the Share button in the upper-right corner of the window. To automatically save your Reading List to read offline, open the Settings app, tap Apps, tap Safari, and turn on Automatically Save Offline.

>> **Search a web page.** Tap the Share button, and then tap Find on Page.

>> **Translate a page.** Tap the Page Settings button, and then tap the Translate button (which appears if translation is available).

Using Safari's Reader Feature

In Safari, you can opt to read websites in Reader mode, which enables you to view the site without advertisements, navigation menus, or other distracting items.

To enabled Reader mode, tap the Page Settings button to the right of the Smart Search field, by pinching your index finger to your thumb, and then do one of the following:

To Do This . . .	Follow These Steps . . .
Show the Reader.	Tap Show Reader.
Always use the Reader for the current website.	Tap Website Settings and then turn on Use Reader Automatically.
Automatically use Reader for all websites that support it.	Open the Settings app, tap Apps, tap Safari, tap Reader, and turn on All Websites.

To return to the full page, tap the Page Settings button and tap Hide Reader.

Note: If Reader is dimmed, Reader isn't available for that web page.

Downloading Files from Safari

You can download a file on Apple Vision Pro to preview it later. To do so, pinch and hold the file or link you want to download by pressing your index finger to your thumb and holding it; then tap Download Linked File.

To see your downloads, tap the Page Settings button on the right side of the Smart Search field, and then tap Downloads.

You can also check the status of a file you're downloading (how much more time it'll take to finish downloading), access downloaded files quickly, or drag a downloaded file onto another file or into an email you're working on.

And just like on a Mac or PC, you can download files in the background while you continue using Safari.

TIP

Did you know you can use keyboard shortcuts with your Magic Keyboard (if you've got one)? If your Apple Vision Pro is connected to your Magic Keyboard via Bluetooth, you can use keyboard shortcuts to navigate in Safari. To view the available keyboard shortcuts, connect your keyboard and then press and hold the ⌘ key.

Chapter **15**

Taking Notes and Making Voice Recordings

M aybe because I'm a journalist, I often use the Notes and Voice Memos apps on my iPhone. Jotting down notes — everything from grocery lists to ideas for new articles or books — is something I do to stay organized in both my personal and professional lives. Voice recordings I tend to use more for work, whether I'm interviewing someone in person for my radio show/podcast or just capturing a few quotes I could use in an article.

You can access the Notes and Voice Memos apps inside Apple Vision Pro, too. And you can synchronize your notes and voice recordings between devices — for example, you might dictate a speech for your friend's wedding while wearing Apple Vision Pro, and then review it later on your iPhone while you're in line at the grocery store.

In this chapter, I cover how to get everything you need out of the Notes and Voice Memos apps.

Using the Notes App

On the main Home View screen, look at the Notes app and pinch your index finger to your thumb to open it. In the Notes app, you should see any previously created notes along the left-hand side, in categories like Notes, Work, Shared, or iCloud (synchronized across all compatible devices when you're signed into the same Apple ID).

Creating and formatting a new note

To create and format a new note, follow these steps:

1. **Tap the New Note button in the upper-right corner (see Figure 15-1).**

2. **Enter your text.**

   Unless you rename the note, the first line will be the title of your note (like "Grocery List" or "Podcast Ideas").

3. **Tap the Format button (which looks like "Aa") to apply a heading style, italic or bold font, a bulleted or numbered list, and more.**

New Note

Courtesy of Apple, Inc.

FIGURE 15-1:
Tap the New Note button to create and view a new note in Apple Vision Pro.

To add more content to your note, you can also:

>> **Add a table.** Tap the Table button, which looks like a small grid.

>> **Add a checklist.** Tap the Checklist button, which looks like a list of items.

>> **Draw or write.** Tap the Handwriting Tools button, which looks like the tip of a marker. Then use the toolbar to choose different tools and colors, select parts of your drawing, and more (see Figure 15-2). Use your fingertip in the air to draw.

>> **Import photos, video, document scans, and more.** Tap the Camera button, and then choose the option you want.

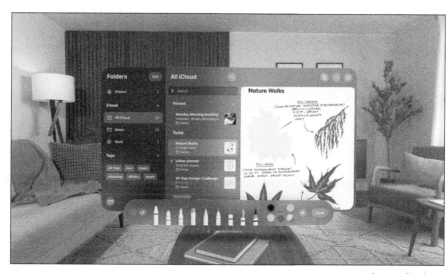

Courtesy of Apple, Inc.

You can also your iPhone to scan documents and take photos on Apple Vision Pro if it's signed in with the same Apple ID. Look at Scan Documents; then tap the name of your iPhone from the list.

Use hashtags as a quick way to organize and find your notes. You can add one or more tags to a note, such as #grocerylist or #work, and easily search and filter your notes across folders.

TIP

To choose a default style for the first line in all new notes, open the Settings app, tap Apps, tap Notes, tap New Notes Start With, and select from the options (Title, Heading, Subheading, or Body).

To delete a note or a folder, swipe left on the note in the sidebar, and then tap the Delete button (which looks like a trash can). Or press and hold on a note or folder for a second or so, and tap Delete.

Adding info to a note from another app

You can add information from another app as an attachment to a note. For example, copy and paste a recipe from a social media app, a location in Maps, an article in the Safari web browser, a PDF in Files, or a screenshot.

In the other app, open the item you want to share (for example, a web page), tap the Share button, and then tap Notes. Now save the item to a new note or choose an existing note.

Locking a note

If you have important information in a note, you can add a virtual padlock to it. Then, when you want to access the locked note, you use your device passcode, a custom passcode of your choosing, or Optic ID.

To choose the password you want to use, open the Settings app, tap Apps, tap Notes, and tap Password. Tap an Apple account (if you have more than one), and then tap Use Device Passcode or Use Custom Passcode.

WARNING

If you forget your custom passcode and you can't use Optic ID to access your locked notes for whatever reason, Apple can't help you regain access to those notes.

To lock a note, open the note and tap the More button; then tap Lock.

SHORTCUTS USING MAGIC KEYBOARD

Assuming you own a Bluetooth-enabled Magic Keyboard and it's wirelessly connected to your Apple Vision Pro, try these shortcuts to save time while inside the Notes app:

- **To start a new note:** Press ⌘+N.
- **To add a checklist:** Press Shift+⌘+L.
- **To create a bulleted list:** Press Shift+⌘+7.
- **To hide the sidebar:** Press Control+⌘+S.

To open a locked note, tap the locked note, and tap View Note. Then use the correct passcode or let Apple Vision Pro scan your eyes for Optic ID.

Sharing notes or collaborating with others

After you create a note, you can easily send it to someone for them to view it. You can even work on a note together, remotely.

To collaborate with others, you can share a note (or a folder of notes) over iCloud. You can set permissions for the other collaborator(s) – like allowing them to edit the note, add attachments like a photo or PDF, and/or create subfolders – and it's cool as you can see what changes are made in real time.

To share a note or folder, follow these steps:

1. **Open the note you want to share.**

2. **Tap the Share button (or pinch and hold the folder you want to share, and tap Share Folder).**

3. **Tap Collaborate.**

   You can't collaborate on a locked note (or on a folder with locked notes).

4. **To change the access and permissions, tap the share options below Collaborate.**

5. **Choose how to send your invitation (for example, using Messages or Mail).**

An orange dot to the left of a note in the notes list (on the left) means the note has changed since you last looked at it. Open the note, and you can swipe right on the note or swipe up on the Activity card to see who made changes (and when).

If you want to adjust how the activity is shown, tap the Participants button, and then choose one of the following:

>> **Show Updates:** Shows changes made since you last opened the note

>> **Show All Activity:** Shows all activity in the note

>> **Show Highlights:** Shows names, dates, and changes made by each collaborator

If you want to mention a collaborator and notify them of important updates, type an @ sign followed by their name, and they'll see the changes.

To view activity in a folder, pinch and hold the folder on the left, and then tap Show Folder Activity.

Changing settings for the Notes app

To change settings for your Notes app on Apple Vision Pro, open the Settings app, tap Apps, tap Notes, and adjust any of the following settings:

>> **Password:** Lock important notes with a custom password.

>> **Default Account:** Choose the default account for Siri (if you have more than one).

>> **Sort Notes By:** Choose Date Edited, Date Created, or Title.

>> **Lines & Grids:** Choose a line or grid style for handwriting in new notes.

>> **Save to Photos:** Save photos and videos taken in Notes to the Photos app.

Using the Voice Memos App

The Voice Memos app lets you get ideas down in a digital format, just by speaking into your device. Whether you're conducting interviews or recording meetings or lectures, you can use the Voice Memos app with surprisingly good audio quality. Musicians also love the Voice Memos app as a quick and easy way to get a melody down — whether it's hummed, sung, or played on a piano or guitar.

Because the Voice Memos app is an iPad app that works with Apple Vision Pro, you can find and use it in the Compatible Apps folder right off your Home View screen.

This portable recorder lets you organize your voice recordings, synchronize them between all compatible devices (as long as you're signed into the same Apple ID and Voice Memos is enabled in iCloud), and take advantage of editing tools like trim, playback speed, skip silence, and resume.

If you aren't seeing your voice memos shared between Apple devices, open the Settings app, tap your name, tap iCloud, tap Show All, and make sure Voice Memos is enabled.

Making a voice recording

After you open the Voice Memos app, to begin recording, simply tap the red Record button by looking at it and tapping your index finger to your thumb.

You can record voice memos using the built-in microphone in Apple Vision Pro or an external microphone, if you have one (such as built into your Apple AirPods).

If you don't want to hear the start and stop tones, turn down the volume on your Apple Vision Pro.

Tap the Pause button to temporarily stop recording; tap Resume to continue. Tap Done to stop recording.

For your privacy, when you're recording a memo, an orange dot appears at the top of your view to indicate your microphone is in use.

Figure 15-3 shows a new voice recording in progress. You'll see a visual reference to the length and volume level.

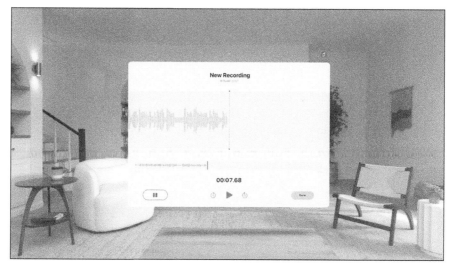

FIGURE 15-3: Recording and playing back voice memos while wearing Apple Vision Pro is quick and easy.

Courtesy of Apple, Inc.

Your new recording is saved with the name New Recording or the name of your location (if Location Services is turned on in the Settings app under Privacy & Security). To change the name of the recording, tap the recording, tap the name, and type a new one.

Tap the recording to play it instantly.

Don't like the recording? Tap Edit at the top of the list of voice recordings, select the voice note(s) you want to delete, and then tap the Delete icon to delete it.

If you need to tweak your recording, open the recording and tap Edit.

Like to multitask? You can use another app while recording a voice memo, as long as that other app doesn't play audio on your Apple Vision Pro. While recording, go to Home View and open another app. If the other app starts playing or recording sound, Voice Memos stops recording.

Playing and editing a voice recording

To play a voice recording, open the Voice Memos app and tap a recording. You'll immediately hear it. The buttons you see while the recording is playing will probably be familiar to you — press Pause to pause the playback, Play to play it again, the Rewind 15 Seconds button to skip back 15 seconds, or the Fast-Forward 15 Seconds button to skip ahead 15 seconds.

TIP

While the recording is open, you can tap its name to rename it.

Alternatively, when a voice note is open, tap the Options icon in the top right of the screen (represented by three horizontal bars), and you can play a recording at a faster or slower speed, and do things like enhance the audio to reduce background noise and echo. You can also have Voice Memos analyze your audio and automatically skip over gaps when playing. Figure 15-4 shows some of the editing options.

FIGURE 15-4:
Musicians can quickly throw down a melody by humming, singing, or playing an instrument — and then they edit the memo later on, in a variety of ways.

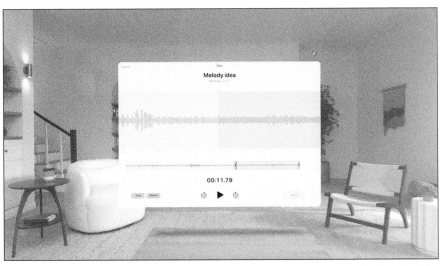

Courtesy of Apple, Inc.

If you want to trim a recording, choose an audio file along the left-hand side, and then tap Edit in the upper right. Tap the Trim button in the upper right, and then pinch and drag the yellow trim handles to enclose the section you want to keep or delete. (You can also zoom in on the waveform for more precise editing.) To keep the selection (and delete the rest of the recording), tap Trim. To delete the selection, tap Delete. When you're done editing, tap Save and then tap Done.

To duplicate or delete a recording, tap the recording, tap the Share button, and then tap Duplicate or Delete. Deleted recordings move to the Recently Deleted folder, where they're kept for up to a month by default (which you can change by opening the Settings app, tapping Apps, tapping Voice Memos, and tapping Clear Deleted).

Finding, organizing, and sharing voice recordings

In the Voice Memos app, you can mark recordings as favorites and organize your recordings into specific folders.

To mark a recording as a favorite, tap the recording in the main list, and then tap the Favorite button above the waveform on the right.

TIP

Favorites, Recently Deleted, and Apple Watch recordings are all grouped into what Apple calls *Smart Folders* (which are folders that automatically gather files by type and subject matter). Along with the automatic Smart Folders, you can also manually group related recordings together into folders to easily locate them. Tap Edit above the list of recordings, and then do any of the following:

>> **Create a folder.** Tap the New Folder button, and then type a name for the folder.

>> **Move recordings to a folder.** Select one or more recordings, and then tap Move.

>> **Delete a folder.** Tap the Delete button next to the folder, and then tap the Trash button.

>> **Change folder order.** Pinch and drag the Reorder button next to any folder.

To search for a voice memo, pinch and swipe down from the middle of the list of recordings to reveal the search field. Then enter part or all of the recording name.

To share a recording with others, tap the recording you want to share, and then tap the Share button to select AirDrop, Messages, Mail, or another option.

Chapter **16**

Getting Stuff Done with Freeform and Keynote

S ure, Apple Vision Pro is a cool device for experiencing immersive videos and playing mixed-reality games, but it's so much more than that! In fact, this revolutionary spatial computer is an exceptional tool for brainstorming and collaborating with colleagues, regardless of where you are. From the hologram-like spatial Personas (see Chapter 6) to fleshing out ideas on a digital whiteboard like Freeform, Apple Vision Pro has you covered.

Freeform lets you organize and visually lay out content on a flexible canvas, giving you the ability to see, share, and collaborate all in one place — without worrying about layouts or page sizes. You can sketch, draw with color, add text and graphs, import photos and videos, and much more, to visualize your work. It's available on iPhone, iPad, and Mac, but it's even more powerful on Apple Vision Pro.

In this chapter, I share how to create and use Freeform boards in Apple Vision Pro. I also fill you in on other productivity-centric tools like mirroring your Apple Vision Pro to a nearby Mac, leveraging Focus to stay in the zone, and creating presentations using Keynote.

Launching and Using the Freeform App in Apple Vision Pro

The built-in Freeform app (shown in Figure 16-1) is a great way to create and share digital whiteboards with colleagues. Freeform can be used for personal projects, too, like planning a home renovation or thinking through a school science project.

FIGURE 16-1:
Apple Vision Pro and the built-in Freeform app are excellent ways to brainstorm and collaborate on ideas — even with people not in the room with you.

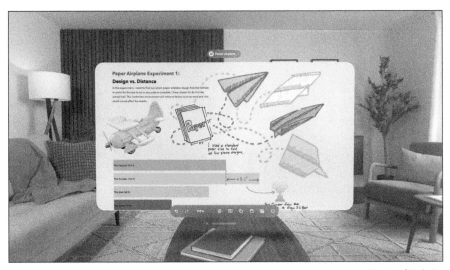

Courtesy of Apple, Inc.

In other words, you can use this giant pinboard in numerous ways. Add drawings (using a variety of brush styles and colors), shapes, photos, video, audio, documents, PDFs, web links, stickies and more — anywhere on a Freeform board.

In the following sections, I walk you through how to use Freeform on Apple Vision Pro.

Creating a new Freeform board

To create a new Freeform board, follow these steps:

1. **From the main Home View screen, look at the Freeform icon and tap your index finger to your thumb to open it.**

2. **Tap the New Board button.**

3. **Tap an option at the bottom of the window to start building your board by selecting markers, shapes, text, and more.**

When wearing Apple Vision Pro, you can use your hands in the air to move around your board. Pinch and hold an empty area of the board and then drag. To zoom in or out, pinch and hold with both hands; then drag your hands apart or together. More gestures for repositioning items on the board are below.

Choose a magnification by tapping the percentage at the bottom of the window.

To name your board, just tap the placeholder name at the top, and then tap Rename.

All your work will be synchronized between your devices over iCloud when you're signed into the same Apple ID (see Figure 16-2). If your work isn't syncing, open the Settings app, tap your name, tap iCloud, and turn on Freeform.

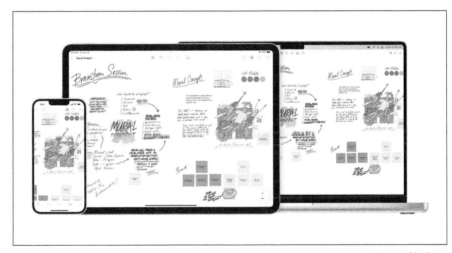

FIGURE 16-2:
As long as you're signed into the same Apple ID on your devices, all your Freeform boards will be conveniently synced across them all.

Courtesy of Apple, Inc.

Opening an existing Freeform board

Top open an existing a Freeform board, you can open it by opening the Freeform app, tapping a category in the sidebar (like Recents or Shared), and tapping the board you want to open.

If you're already working in a Freeform board and you want to open another one, tap the name of your board at the top and then tap Open.

Boards you worked on most recently are at the top of the screen. To make it easy to find a board, you can change how boards are sorted by tapping the Grid View button or the List View button.

You can also make a board a favorite by pinching and holding the board, and then tapping Favorite (or tap the name of the board at the top of the window and then tap Favorite while you're working on a board). Your favorites now appear in the sidebar while browsing.

Duplicating a Freeform board

If you want to duplicate a board (to keep one as is but modify another further), while browsing All Boards tap Select in the upper-right corner of the window and then tap the board you want to copy and tap Duplicate. Alternatively, pinch and hold the thumbnail or name of the board and then tap Duplicate.

If you duplicate a shared board, the copy isn't shared.

Deleting a Freeform board

To delete a board, while browsing All Boards, tap Select in the upper-right corner, then tap and hold on a board you want to delete, and tap Delete.

To quickly delete a single board, you can pinch and hold the board, tap Delete, and then tap Delete at the lower-right corner of the window.

If you deleted a board by mistake, don't worry! You can recover recently deleted boards for up to 30 days by tapping Recently Deleted in the sidebar, and then tap Recover.

Positioning items on a Freeform board

When you're working on a Freeform board, you can do a number of gesture-based actions to move items on your board, resize or group item, and lock them into place. The Freeform board will automatically accommodate any new items you place on it, even as you move items beyond the edges of the board.

Table 16-1 outlines the gestures you'll want to learn.

TABLE 16-1   ## Helpful Keynote Gestures

To Do This . . .	Do This Gesture . . .
Select an item.	Tap the item by looking at it and then touching your index finger to your thumb.
Select multiple items.	Tap the Select Multiple Objects button and then tap each item.
Move an item.	Pinch the item and drag it.
Group items.	Select the dotted circle icon in the lower right of the screen and then tap Select All. With multiple items selected, tap the Arrange button, and then tap an alignment option or Group.
Rotate an item.	Pinch the item with both hands and then turn your hands in the direction you want the object to rotate.
Put an item in the background or foreground.	Tap the object, tap the More button, and then tap Back or Front.
Resize an item.	Tap an item, and then pinch and drag a blue dot. In text boxes, drag a green dot to resize both the box and the text within it.
Lock an item.	To prevent an item from being moved or formatted, tap the item, tap the More button, and tap Lock.

TIP

Guides can help you place items precisely. They appear as you drag an item on a board in alignment with another item. You can turn the guides off and on as needed. Open the Settings app, tap Apps, tap Freeform, and then turn Center Guides, Edge Guides, and Spacing Guides on or off.

To add shapes and lines in a Freeform board, tap the Add Shape button, and then select a shape or line type. You can find lines, curves, and arrows on the Basic tab. To add a text box or sticky note, tap the Add Text Box button or the Add Sticky Note button. To show formatting tools, tap the text box or sticky note. You can change the font, alignment, sticky note color, use list formatting, and more.

To draw on a Freeform board, tap the Drawing and Handwriting Tool button, and then pinch and hold to draw. You can switch tools as needed (see Figure 16-3). Tap the tool a second time to see if there are additional options, like stroke size (line thickness) or transparency.

You can also select, copy, and delete sections of a drawing. When you finish draw-ing, your strokes are grouped. If you want to break a drawing apart, you can regroup your strokes, or separate, delete, or resize them. On a Freeform board, tap the Lasso tool in the drawing toolbar. Tap or circle the part of the drawing you want to select, and then choose an option.

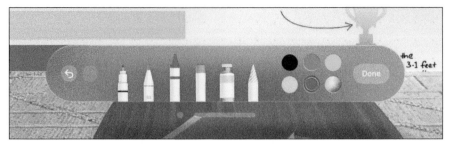

Courtesy of Apple, Inc.

TIP

In Freeform, you can provide an accessible description to any item on your board, so an explanation of the visual content is spoken aloud when someone uses assistive technology, such as Apple's VoiceOver, to access your board. (Descriptions aren't visible on the board itself.) To add an accessible description, follow these steps:

1. Select an item.

2. Tap the More button.

3. Tap the Image Inspector button.

4. Tap Description.

5. Enter a description of the visual content.

6. Tap Done.

To hear the description, turn on VoiceOver by opening the Settings app, tapping Accessibility, and tapping VoiceOver; then tap the item.

Collaborating on a Freeform board

You can use the Freeform app by yourself, but it's great to work on a Freeform board with other people. And they don't need to be wearing Apple Vision Pro either — the Freeform app also works with iPhone, iPad, and Mac.

When you're in the Freeform app, it's easy to invite people to collaborate on a board over iCloud. That way, everyone will see the latest changes when they're online and signed in with their Apple ID. Just follow these steps:

1. Open Freeform and open a board.

2. Tap the name of the board at the top.

3. Tap the Share Board button.

4. **Type the name of the person or people who you want to be able to access the board, the level of access you want them to have (such as only view but not edit), and how you want to send the link (such as via Messages or Mail).**

   When you share a board via the Messages app, you can see who made updates since the last time you viewed the board in Messages.

To make changes after you start sharing, tap the Collaboration button, and then tap Manage Shared Board. When you stop sharing, the board will no longer appear on the devices of the other participants, but you'll still have access to it.

TIP

If you want to see when others are working on the board in real time, you can tap the Collaboration button, and then turn on Participant Cursors. If you're collaborating with people using an iPhone, iPad, or Mac, Participant Cursors may not be available.

If you want to share your Freeform project with someone who isn't on an Apple device, you can export your work and send a PDF copy of a board to them to look at. Head to "Exporting a Freeform board," later in this chapter, for more information.

You can also collaborate on a Freeform board during a call, such as in a FaceTime video chat, so you can see each other and work on the board together in real time. Here's how:

1. **During a FaceTime call, tap Not Shared above the window.**

2. **Tap SharePlay.**

3. **If you just want others on the call to see your window, tap Share My Entire Window.**

4. **To stop sharing, tap SharePlay and then tap Stop Sharing.**

If you want to show a board alongside other windows, you can also share your entire view.

Exporting a Freeform board

To export a PDF copy of a board you've been working on:

1. **Open the board you want to share.**

2. **Tap the Actions Menu button.**

3. **Tap Export as PDF.**

4. **Choose how you want to share the board, such as Mail, AirDrop, or Messages, and follow the instructions by selecting a recipient.**

TIP

People (and groups of people) you've chatted with recently will appear as icons, which you can also tap for extra convenience.

Seeing Your Mac Screen while Using Apple Vision Pro

A feature called Mac Virtual Display lets you view your Mac screen on Apple Vision Pro (see Figure 16-4). You can even use your Mac trackpad to share the pointer between your Mac and Apple Vision Pro. This feature could really help boost your productivity by enabling you to access both devices simultaneously! New updates will be added to Mac Virtual Display throughout 2024, including an increase in resolution.

FIGURE 16-4:
A video being edited on Mac Virtual Display.

Courtesy of Apple, Inc.

To get going, you need a few things:

» Both your Apple Vision Pro and Mac computer must be signed in with the same Apple ID.

>> Both devices need to be on the same Wi-Fi network with Bluetooth enabled and within range of each other (typically 30 feet).

>> Your Mac must have macOS Sonoma or later installed. (Sonoma debuted in September 2023.)

>> Both devices need iCloud Keychain turned on. To turn on iCloud Keychain on your Mac, open System Settings, tap your name, tap iCloud, tap Passwords & Keychain, and turn on Sync This Mac. To turn on iCloud Keychain on your Apple Vision Pro, open the Settings app, tap your name, tap iCloud, tap Passwords & Keychain, and turn on Sync This Apple Vision Pro.

To connect to your Mac, while wearing Apple Vision Pro, open Control Center, tap the expanded Control Center icon (which looks like two oval shapes with a button inside of each of them), tap the Mac Virtual Display button, and choose your Mac. Alternatively, if you're using a MacBook, you may be able to simply look at your MacBook (make sure the Mac display is on) and tap the Connect button.

You can change the size of the Mac screen and move it toward or away from you. Simply pinch and drag the window bar at the bottom side to side, toward you, or away from you. To resize an app, look at the lower-right or lower-left corner of the app window, and pinch and drag the resize control.

While you're connected, use your trackpad with your Mac as you normally would. You can also move the pointer past the edge of the Mac screen until it appears in an open visionOS app (and vice versa). You can also continue using gestures to work with your visionOS apps!

To disconnect Mac Virtual Display, tap the Close button.

TIP

A few things to note:

>> If your Mac has multiple displays connected to it, Mac Virtual Display shows only the one that you've set as the main display.

>> To adjust the resolution of your Mac display in Apple Vision Pro, open the System Settings app on your Mac, click Displays, and choose from the available resolutions. To see more sizes, turn on Show All Resolutions.

   If you have a Mac with Apple silicon (like an AM1, M2, or M3 chip), it can appear in Apple Vision Pro at resolutions up to 4K. If your Mac has an Intel processor, it can appear at resolutions up to 3K.

>> If you want to share the pointer between your macOS and visionOS apps, Handoff must be turned on for both devices. On Apple Vision Pro, open the Settings app, tap General, and tap Handoff. On your Mac, open the System

Settings app, tap General, and tap AirDrop & Handoff. On your Mac, you also need to open the System Settings app, click General, and click AirDrop & Handoff; also in the System Settings app, click Displays, click Advanced, and turn on Allow Your Pointer and Keyboard to Move between Any Nearby Mac or iPad.

REMEMBER

You can also mirror your Apple Vision Pro view on another screen so others can see what you see inside the headset! You can do this with an iPhone, iPad, Apple TV, compatible smart TV, or Mac. To share your view, open Control Center, then tap the expanded Control Center button, tap the Mirror My View button, and choose a compatible device from the list of available devices (like your nearby Mac). You need to be logged into the same Apple ID on both devices and the two devices must be using the same Wi-Fi network.

Using Keynote on Apple Vision Pro

One of the more popular presentation tools is available in Apple Vision Pro. In fact, it's preloaded! (And yes, Microsoft PowerPoint is also available at the App Store for Apple Vision Pro, if you prefer.)

In this chapter, however, I explain how to create, view, and share amazingly visual presentations in Keynote (see Figure 16-5). And hey, you can even rehearse presentations in an Apple Vision Pro Environment (see Chapter 4) like Conference Room or Theater!

FIGURE 16-5:
If you ever have to give a presentation, take advantage of the integrated Keynote app inside of Apple Vision Pro.

Courtesy of Apple, Inc.

To get started with Keynote on Apple Vision Pro:

1. **Open Keynote from the Home View by looking at the Keynote icon and tapping your index finger to your thumb.**

2. **To create a Keynote presentation, start with a theme, and then modify it however you like after that.**

   Individual slides in a theme include placeholder images and text, which vary based on the style of the presentation you chose.

3. **Build your presentation by replacing the placeholder content with your own content.**

   You can also delete placeholders you don't want. A toolbar at the bottom of the app also lets you add objects to your text, such as charts, photos, or shapes. You can also add 3D objects, and edit and view them, inside your presentation.

   When you select an object — such as a shape, chart, table, or cell — you'll see formatting controls in the format bar (for the type of object you selected). You can also use the controls in the navigation bar at the top of the screen (like Format or the More button) for extra formatting and presentation options.

Keynote automatically saves your presentation as you work. If iCloud is set up, the presentation is saved there by default, which means it's also synced between all your compatible Apple devices.

You can also rename a presentation. To do so, tap the presentation name near the top of the window, tap Rename, type a new name, and tap Rename. That's it!

To make a copy of a presentation:

1. **Open Keynote.**

2. **Open a presentation.**

3. **Tap the name of the presentation at the top.**

4. **Tap Open to see all your presentations.**

5. **Pinch and hold the thumbnail of the presentation you want to copy.**

6. **Tap Duplicate.**

   The duplicate presentation appears with a number appended to its name, like "Marc's XYZ Speech (2)."

Rehearsing your Keynote presentation

Rehearsing your Keynote presentation in an Environment, as shown in Figure 16-6, is a great way to practice before the big day! You can even control the lights, adjust the volume of the Environment sounds, and more. (Plus, I cover Environments in greater depth in Chapter 4.)

FIGURE 16-6: On Apple Vision Pro, you can rehearse your Keynote presentation in a realistic setting, like a conference room or a theater, and see your presentation on the screen in the Environment.

Courtesy of Apple, Inc.

To rehearse your presentation:

1. **Open the presentation.**

2. **Tap to select the first slide in the slide navigator on the left.**

3. **Tap the Rehearse Presentation button.**

4. **Choose an Environment.**

   Note that Environments have their own sounds that suit the setting you chose. To turn down the volume, turn the Digital Crown above your right eye, and look at the Volume icon while you turn.

Here's what you can do in an Environment:

>> To go to the next slide, look at the slides on the presenter display (or the virtual screen where your presentation is displayed), and tap or swipe left.

>> To go back a slide, look at the slides on the presenter display (or the virtual screen where your presentation is displayed), and tap or swipe right.

>> To move and customize the presenter display, pinch and drag the window bar below the display, tap the Arrange button, and then tap a layout option.

>> In the Conference Room Environment, switch positions by tapping the More button, tapping Rehearsal Settings, and choosing an option.

>> Turn the lights up or down by tapping the More button and then tapping Lights Up or Lights Down.

>> To change the Environment, tap the More button, and then tap Environment.

>> To show a laser pointer, tap the Illustrator button, and then pinch and hold to show a laser pointer on the slide.

To stop rehearsing, tap the Minimize button.

Sending or collaborating on a Keynote speech

Like most apps in Apple Vision Pro, you can also collaborate (and even present) with others not with you.

First, you'll need to invite them to work with you on your presentation. Everyone you invite can see changes as they're made, but you control who can edit or only view the presentation. Send a copy of a Keynote presentation using Mail, AirDrop, Messages, or another service, or you can collaborate on the presentation with others using iCloud.

TIP

Before you send your presentation to someone, you can password-protect it to restrict access to the presentation and provide extra security. To do so, tap the More button in the navigation bar at the top of the window, tap Presentation Options, and tap Set Password.

To send a copy of your presentation:

1. **Tap the Share button in the navigation bar at the top of the window.**

2. **Tap Send Copy.**

3. **Choose how to send it (like Mail or Messages).**

4. **Tap the More button to add another service to the options.**

   You may need to swipe to see the More button.

5. **Tap Export and Send.**

You can also send a copy when you export to PowerPoint or another file format, such as PDF, Microsoft PowerPoint, Movie, and more. Tap the More button and then tap Export.

To collaborate on an open presentation:

1. **Tap the Share button.**

2. **Tap Collaborate.**

To share a folder in iCloud Drive, pinch and hold it, then tap Share Folder. To change the access and permissions, tap the share options below Collaborate.

If you send the invitation in Messages, you get activities updates in the Messages conversation when someone makes changes in the shared presentation. Tap the updates to go to the shared presentation.

Edits you and others make to the Keynote presentation appear in real time, including insertion points and selections of text and objects, which will appear in different colors to indicate where others are currently editing. If you don't want to see these real-time updates, tap the Collaborate button and turn off Participant Cursors.

TIP

If you see a message that you're offline, that's okay. You can continue to work on the Keynote presentation, and the next time you're online, changes will be uploaded to iCloud automatically.

If you have an external keyboard connected to your Apple Vision Pro, you can use keyboard shortcuts to quickly accomplish many tasks in Keynote. Press and hold the Command key on the keyboard to show a list of shortcuts for the Keynote item that's selected on the slide, like text or a table. To use a keyboard shortcut, press all the keys in the shortcut at the same time.

Using Focus with Apple Vision Pro

Minimizing distractions while you're trying to work is easy on Apple Vision Pro. In fact, it's not just for working — any time you want to focus on a specific activity, you can customize one of the provided Focus options inside the headset (for instance, Work, Personal, or Sleep, or a Custom Focus). This is similar to Focus on some other Apple devices, like iPhone. Figure 16-7 shows what it looks like in Apple Vision Pro.

FIGURE 16-7:
Focus settings on Apple Vision Pro, showing options to set up a focus, share across your devices, and share Focus status.

To set up a Focus:

1. **Open the Settings app, tap Focus, and tap a Focus.**

    I'll use Work as an example here, given this is a chapter on productivity.

2. **Specify which apps and people (like coworkers or family members) can send you notifications during your Focus.**

3. **You can also schedule the Focus to turn on when you're at a certain location, at a certain time of day, and so on.**

TIP

Use the same Focus settings on all your Apple devices where you're signed in with the same Apple ID. If it's not on by default, open the Settings app, tap Focus, and then turn on Share across Devices. That way, you won't get notifications on your iPhone when you're trying to work on your Apple Vision Pro.

You have a few options with Focus:

>> You can allow apps to send time-sensitive notifications by turning on — you guessed it — Time Sensitive Notifications. This could be something like a medication reminder app.

>> If people are calling you repeatedly, you can turn on Allow Repeated Calls. That way, you won't miss something truly urgent.

>> You can create a list of allowed or silenced people or apps.

When you turn on Focus in Apple Vision Pro, it limits the notifications you receive from certain apps and people. When someone outside your allowed app and people notifications attempt to contact you, your Focus status appears in Messages, so they know you're busy and don't want to be disturbed. Focus status is shared in apps if you give an app permission to see your Focus status. Open the Settings app, tap Focus, tap Focus Status, turn on Share Focus Status, then select the options you want.

TIP

To quickly silence all notifications, open Control Center, tap the expanded Control Center button, tap the Focus button, and turn on Do Not Disturb.

To delete a Focus, open the Settings app, tap Focus, tap the Focus you want to delete, and tap Delete Focus. If you delete a provided Focus and change your mind, you have to set it up again from scratch.

5

The Part of Tens

IN THIS PART . . .

Discover the ten most amazing things you can do in Apple Vision Pro, for work or for play.

Explore the very best third-party apps to help you get the most out of Apple's revolutionary device.

IN THIS CHAPTER

» Capturing and viewing spatial images

» Experiencing immersive content

» FaceTiming with your Persona and multitasking with spatial Personas

» Playing mixed-reality games

» Sharing your view to another device

» Practicing mindfulness

Chapter **17**

Ten Awesome Things to Try in Apple Vision Pro

Whether you've already read most of the book or you jumped right to The Part of Tens (a fan favorite), you've landed in a chapter with my ten picks for the most awesome things you can do in Apple Vision Pro!

From capturing and viewing spatial photos and videos, to playing games with gestures in the air, to experiencing incredibly immersive videos, or using Personas and spatial Personas, this a top-ten list that can't be beat.

Capturing Spatial Photos and Videos

One of the coolest ways to experience Apple's spatial computer is to capture photos and videos in incredibly realistic 3D depth and detail, and then play back the images in Apple Vision Pro to be magically whisked back to that exact moment. See Figure 17-1 for a simulated look at spatial images.

FIGURE 17-1:
Relive
memories
with incredible
depth and
detail inside
the Apple
Vision Pro
headset.

Courtesy of Apple, Inc.

If you own an iPhone 15 Pro or iPhone 15 Pro Max (or newer), you can also capture spatial images using that device and then play it back later in the headset. And a special lens from Canon is coming soon, too (at the time of this writing)!

Also coming soon, Apple Intelligence (Apple's version of AI) will be able to turn a regular ol' 2D photo into a 3D spatial one.

TIP

For all the details on how to use Apple Vision Pro to capture a spatial photo or video, turn to Chapter 13.

Viewing Immersive Content and 3D Videos

Why watch regular ol' 2D video content when you can do so much more with Apple Vision Pro? The Apple TV app in Apple Vision Pro allows you to watch Apple Immersive Videos, which are 180-degree 8K recordings, captured with spatial audio, which puts you in the middle of the action. Plus, you can buy or rent 3D movies in the Apple TV app.

TIP

For info on how to use Apple Vision Pro to watch immersive content, head to Chapter 9.

Using Personas to FaceTime

FaceTiming on Apple Vision Pro is really fun! You're represented by a scan of yourself called a Persona, which is what the other person sees. Even though you digitize your appearance only once (unless you want to redo it), your mouth movement, facial expressions, and upper-body motions are mapped to your Persona in real time, so the person you're FaceTiming with still sees "you" (more or less). If you're talking with someone who is *not* on Apple Vision Pro, you see a 2D video of them, which you can pin to a part of the environment you're in, and even chat with them while doing something together, like editing a Freeform board or playing a heated game of Chess via the SharePlay feature.

Spatial Personas are even cooler — they're like a hologram of the person you're chatting with, so it feels like you're together in the same room. You can make eye contact, point at something and look at something together, like a video.

TIP

For info on how to FaceTime on Apple Vision Pro with your spatial Persona, turn to Chapter 6.

Playing Mixed-Reality Games

I'd argue that Apple Vision Pro isn't as much for gamers as other headsets, like Meta Quest 3, are — but you *can* download games from the App Store. And some of those games take advantage of Apple Vision's Pro's *passthrough* capabilities, which enable you to see both digital content and the world around you at the same time.

For example, the quirky Super Fruit Ninja lets you slice fruits with your hands. It's fast-paced and a good workout game for the Apple Vision Pro.

And then there's LEGO Builder's Journey (see Figure 17-2), which fuses brick-building fun with a story about connections and adventure.

Other compatible games, like Apple Arcade's NBA 2K23 Arcade Edition, is pretty much the same experience as on an iPhone or iPad, with a Bluetooth controller in your hands, but you can stretch and place the game window wherever you like in the room you're in.

SharePlay games are even cooler, because you can play a game with someone else and see their spatial Persona across from you, as if you were in the same room!

FIGURE 17-2:
LEGO Builder's
Journey is a
"poetic puzzler"
that brings the
bricks to life,
rendered in 3D
in front of you,
accompanied
by a beautiful
soundtrack.

Courtesy of LEGO Systems A/S

For more information on gaming with Apple Vision Pro, turn to Chapter 12.

TIP

Sharing Your Apple Vision Pro View to Another Display

Even though you're the one wearing Apple Vision Pro and having all the fun, you can share what you're seeing and doing in the headset, if there's a compatible device nearby for others to see — like a Mac, iPad, or select smart TV.

To share your Apple Vision Pro view to an external display, turn to Chapter 16.

REMEMBER

You must be signed into the same Apple ID on the other device as your Apple Vision Pro and logged into the same Wi-Fi network. You may need to enter your password and/or accept the Apple Vision Pro's incoming screen mirroring request on your other device. And if the Apple Vision Pro content looks blurry on the external display, it's because the video from your headset can be shared to the outside display at only up to 720p resolution. You may also find limitations in some apps, such as not sharing copyrighted content.

Practicing Mindfulness

The Mindfulness app on Apple Vision Pro encourages you to set aside a few minutes a day to focus on yourself, via various breathing and reflection exercises (see Figure 17-3).

FIGURE 17-3:
The Mindfulness app on Apple Vision Pro, showing options to start a session.

To start a Mindfulness session, follow these steps:

1. **From the main Home View screen on Apple Vision Pro, look at the Mindfulness app (it looks like a teal-colored orb), and press your index finger to your thumb to open it.**

2. **Choose your preferred personal trainer (like Jessica Skye or Christian Howard) and duration of the session by choosing the option on the left side of the screen, or choose Self-Guided session.**

3. **Tap the Start button on the right.**

   Your view gradually gets darker at the start of your session, regardless of your immersion level or Environment settings. If you're in a guided session, listen to the voice and focus on what they instruct you to focus on, including your breathing, the pulsating orb you're seeing, and so on. It's remarkably relaxing.

   During a Mindfulness session, you can tap to see the time elapsed and other options or do any of the following:

- **Change the volume.** Tap the Volume button, and then pinch and drag the slider. You can also turn the Digital Crown to adjust the volume.

- **Pause the session.** Tap the Pause button to pause the session. To resume, tap the Play button.

- **Turn on captions.** Tap the Closed Captions button and then choose a language. To turn off captions, choose Off.

- **End the session.** Tap End.

When your session ends (or you manually end your session by tapping the X), your summary is displayed, including the Mindful Minutes you practiced in this session and the total Mindful Minutes you've practiced this week.

Reading Books

I love reading, and unlike my wife, Kellie, who prefers holding a paperback or hardcover, I'm perfectly good with an e-reader or tablet in my hands. But I wasn't sure how I'd like reading with a headset on my face. Good news: It's surprisingly awesome!

You can comfortably read books in Apple Vision Pro. The text is crisp, it houses an intuitive store (with audiobook support, too), and there are fun features to take advantage of, like highlighting, sharing passages, and changing the layout.

TIP

For tips on buying and reading books (and reading your own PDFs) in Apple Vision Pro, turn to Chapter 11.

Enabling Environments

In Apple Vision Pro, Environments let you transform your physical surroundings into a different place — the Moon, Yosemite, Haleakala in Hawaii, or White Sands in southern New Mexico — while you're inside most apps like Mail, Safari, and Apple TV (excluding games and some immersive video experiences). In Figure 17-4, the Keynote app (Apple's version of PowerPoint) is visible, and an Environment is showing in the background.

In fact, some apps — like Disney+ and Keynote — have exclusive Environments to take advantage of. For example, you can seeing *Star Wars* imagery or a conference room to practice your speech in, respectively (although it would be pretty cool to see *Star Wars* imagery during your presentation).

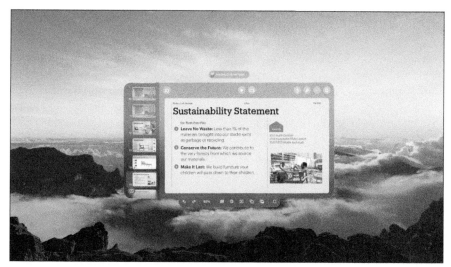

FIGURE 17-4:
Environments
are visible even
when you're
inside some
other apps.

Courtesy of Apple, Inc.

For info on how to choose an Environment, turn to Chapter 4.

TIP

Playing Steam Games

Serious gamers know that much of the action is at the Steam digital store, which lets you download and play several thousand titles on your computer — or via the Steam Link app — while on the same Wi-Fi network. Apple Vision Pro is no exception.

The Steam Link iPad app works on Apple Vision Pro, so you can download it on your headset, log into your Steam account, grab a wireless Bluetooth controller, and play your favorite Steam games while wearing Apple Vision Pro.

It's a little trickier for virtual reality (VR) games, but a free app called Air Light VR (ALVR) can help. You can find ALVR at the App Store. More info is available at `https://github.com/polygraphene/ALVR`.

TIP

Collaborating in Style

This pick isn't tied to one particular app — instead, it's about how Apple Vision Pro enables you to work in real time with others who aren't physically with you, whether they're also on Apple Vision Pro or not.

Especially given our hybrid work setup these days, in which tens of millions of people are working remotely (or a couple of days a week), collaborating on projects is important, so many of the integrated apps in Apple Vision Pro support simultaneous teamwork.

This is especially true with spatial Personas, discussed earlier in this chapter, but even without that, fleshing out ideas is easy in Keynote, Freeform, Messages, or FaceTime (as well as third-party apps that work in Apple Vision Pro, such as Zoom, Teams, Webex, or Slack). And don't forget: In Apple Vision Pro, you can pin other apps in your real-world environment. For example, Figure 17-5 shows someone working on a Keynote presentation while also FaceTiming with two people.

FIGURE 17-5: Apple Vision Pro is a multitasker's dream — you can have multiple windows open at the same time.

Courtesy of Apple, Inc.

The process for inviting someone to collaborate depends on the app, but here's one way you might start a collaboration in a supported app:

1. **Open the app and select the file you want to share.**

2. **Tap Share or Collaborate.**

3. **Make sure Collaborate is selected, and then tap the group or individual you want to collaborate with.**

   If you don't see the group or person listed, start typing a name. The suggested icons are likely individuals or groups you recently communicated with.

Chapter **18**

The Ten Best Apps for Apple Vision Pro

I n this chapter, I recommend ten amazing third-party apps (apps not created by Apple) to download on your Apple Vision Pro. These apps range from games to videos to productivity and more.

Apple Vision Pro is still new (as of this writing). It's exciting to think of what's to come in another few months, let alone years!

REMEMBER

Listed in alphabetical order, here are my top apps to install and run on Apple Vision Pro.

AmazeVR Concerts: Immersive 3D

As a music lover, I couldn't get enough of the Alicia Keys: Rehearsal Room Apple Immersive Video (see Chapter 9). So I was thrilled to discover even *more* amazing musical and spatial experiences with AmazeVR Concerts: Immersive 3D.

With artists like Avenged Sevenfold, Megan Thee Stallion, T-Pain, UPSAHL, and Zara Larsson, these special performances fuse the thrill of live concerts with the magic of a seemingly "personal" show, put on just for you.

For every artist available, you get a free song. If you want more, you can purchase the full concert to watch whenever you like. The footage is shot with a special virtual-reality camera (for left- and right-eye video), in 8K resolution, and up close and personal, so it feels like the performers are right in front of you — including making eye contact. You can even use hand gestures to send love back to the artists!

CARROT Weather: Alerts & Radar

People are obsessed with the weather, so it's no surprise that a handful of weather apps are already available for Apple Vision Pro.

One of the best is CARROT Weather: Alerts & Radar, an iPad app that works with Apple Vision Pro. It dishes up accurate — yet hilarious — forecasts with five personalities to choose from. You'll literally LOL at the meteorological reports while the app gives you real-time weather data and forecasts for your location, with impressive graphics and easy-to-read details on the floating augmented reality (AR) content hovering in front of you.

The free version gives you quite a bit, but a premium subscription offers a lot more, including game-like elements, achievements to unlock, the ability to record your own TV news–style weather report videos, additional customization options, and more.

CellWalk

This free app is proof that biology is fascinating! With CellWalk, Apple Vision Pro users can explore a 3D cell — down to its individual atoms. You can engage in a guided walkthrough or explore on your own with gesture-based controls. The app lets you touch and learn about the cell's important functions. CellWalk is great for students and educators alike!

djay – DJ App & AI Mixer

This virtual DJ app — which debuted when Apple Vision Pro did in early 2024 — delivers a fun, powerful, and interactive DJ experience (see Figure 18-1). Connect your Apple Music account (subscription required) to access more than 100 million songs, as well as other services (like Beatsource, SoundCloud, and TIDAL) and your own personal music library. Take advantage of the virtual turntables, authentic mixing controls, and advanced tools like video mixing, AI features to help you create amazing mixes, and support for real hardware integration.

FIGURE 18-1: Whether you're spinning alone or in a room full of friends, djay is a blast for music lovers.

Courtesy of Algoriddim GmbH.

You can start using this app for free, but you can unlock the djay Pro content for a few bucks a month (prices vary depending on your country).

As shown in Figure 18-1, your virtual gear is seen in front of you, which is a less expensive hobby that buying real DJ equipment!

JigSpace: 3D Presentations

Create and present spatial presentations (or Jigs, as this app calls them) with the free JigSpace: 3D Presentations app. Combining 3D content with audio, video, and text, you can deliver fascinating presentations to communicate ideas, show step-by-step instructions, and teach the inner workings of products in a powerful and interactive manner.

As shown in Figure 18-2, your Jigs look and feel like you're actually demoing with real products, thanks to Apple Vision Pro's capabilities. The app even supports high-resolution 4K textures and computer-aided design (CAD) files.

FIGURE 18-2:
Give lifelike 3D
presentations
with the
JigSpace: 3D
Presentations
app.

Courtesy of JigSpace, Inc.

The app also supports SharePlay, so you can virtually share a room with others while giving a presentation.

MLB

The number-one app for baseball fans is now available for Apple Vision Pro. The MLB app is your gateway to the MLB streaming service to catch Major League Baseball games, in video or audio, available live or on demand. (A subscription to the MLB streaming service is required.) You can jump directly onto your favorite team's tab to see schedules and play content, read news, watch highlights, and receive real-time alerts for your favorite players.

You can pin your screen in your real-world environment, so while wearing Apple Vision Pro, you can kick back and catch all the action, and even multitask (for example, browsing the web at the same time in another pinned window). Or you can choose to hear audio in the background while you're working on something.

Other features include the ability to watch select Minor League Baseball games (via the MLB At Bat service), search through millions of videos in the MLB Film Room, and more.

Puzzling Places

If you like jigsaw puzzles, you'll love Puzzling Places for Apple Vision Pro (see Figure 18-3). This meditative 3D puzzler challenges you to put together photorealistic miniatures of real places from around the world, like churches and castles, using your hands in the air to rotate and piece together puzzles that are seemingly hovering in the real room you're in. While completing puzzles, you'll hear soothing soundscapes for each building you construct. With puzzles ranging from 25 to 200 pieces, a handy autosave feature means you can leave the game and come back to continue at any time.

FIGURE 18-3:
Puzzling Places
brings jigsaw
puzzles to
the spatial
computing
scene.

Courtesy of Realities.io, Inc.

Puzzling Pieces is a freemium game. There is no cost to download and start playing, but optional in-game content is available to purchase after you complete the first three free puzzles.

Sky Guide

Apple Vision Pro already delivers a stellar experience, but it can be even *more* amazing when you look up at the night sky.

On Apple Vision Pro, Sky Guide has you look to the heavens and through AR, it superimposes images and information onto the real sky to tell you what's where — even if it's not visible to the naked eye (see Figure 18-4). Pinpoint stars, planets, moons, and constellations — and receive notifications when the International Space Station is about to fly over your exact location!

Courtesy of Fifth Star Labs, LLC

FIGURE 18-4: Be amazed while marveling at the sky with the free Sky Guide for Apple Vision Pro.

This free app is packed with info and attractive graphics, a personalized calendar of events, historical information, and support for hand gestures and binoculars. And because you're using it outside, it doesn't need Wi-Fi to work!

What If. . .? An Immersive Story

Disney was one of the first major companies to support Apple Vision Pro with its Disney+ app to watch streaming TV shows and movies (see Chapter 9) and exclusive Environments (see Chapter 4).

And now, the media powerhouse has created What If. . .? An Immersive Story, an original tale based on the popular Marvel Studios animated TV series and exclusively available to Apple Vision Pro (see Figure 18-5).

Courtesy of Disney.

Fusing virtual reality (VR) with AR, Marvel fans can travel through the multiverse to iconic worlds (and some new ones, too), along with The Watcher, and fight villains alongside other heroes with the help of the Infinity Stones. Cast spells, unlock new elements to the story, and enjoy 3D stereoscopic videos with smoothly animated characters and effects.

Zoom Workplace

Apple may prefer that you use FaceTime and Freeform for video communication and whiteboarding, respectively, but popular platforms like Zoom are supported in Apple Vision Pro.

Zoom Workplace is a communication and collaboration platform that combines a few services — team chat, scheduled meetings, phone calls over Wi-Fi, digital whiteboarding, calendar, email, notes, and much more.

Available for both free and paid accounts, this single app looks and works great in Apple Vision Pro, with customizable video windows to place around your real environment. Plus, for added convenience, you can receive automated meeting summaries with the Zoom AI Companion feature.

Glossary

3D movies: Films with a lifelike, three-dimensional quality for added depth and immersion.

AirDrop: Using point-to-point Wi-Fi, Apple's AirDrop is a fast and efficient way to wirelessly transfer data between two devices, such as sending photos from Apple Vision Pro to an iPhone, iPad, or Mac.

app: Short for *application,* an app is a computer program that runs on a device or in the cloud. *See also* cloud.

Apple ID: The account you use to access all Apple services. Your Apple ID allows your Apple devices and apps to work together seamlessly.

Apple Vision Pro: Apple's wearable mixed reality or spatial computing headset. *See also* mixed reality (MR) *and* spatial computing.

AR: *See* augmented reality (AR).

augmented reality (AR): A technology that superimposes a computer-generated image on a user's view of the real world.

cloud: Accessed over the internet, the cloud is a distributed collection of servers (a computing system) that host software and infrastructure to access remotely.

Digital Crown: A twistable button on the top right of Apple Vision Pro (above the right eye) that performs various functions when you turn it.

Environment: On Apple Vision Pro, an Environment lets you transform your physical surroundings into a different place — like Yosemite, White Sands, Mount Hood, or the Moon — which you can use in select apps while wearing Apple Vision Pro.

eye tracking: A key feature in Apple Vision Pro's interface that enables you to navigate the device by simply moving your eyes and looking at an object, such as an app icon. visionOS knows what you're looking at. *See also* visionOS.

EyeSight: EyeSight reveals your eyes on the front of your Apple Vision Pro headset and lets those nearby know when you're using apps or fully immersed in an experience.

FaceTime: An exclusive Apple platform that lets users make video or audio calls over the internet.

Fit Dial: Available on the Solo Knit Band that goes around an Apple Vision Pro user's head, the Fit Dial on the right side of the band lets you adjust Apple Vision Pro to your head (tightening or loosening it) and enables micro adjustments during use.

gesture control: By waving your hands around in the air in front of you while you wear an Apple Vision Pro, content is manipulated as if it were controlled by a mouse and keyboard. To select or click, you tap your index finger to your thumb.

head tracking: In Apple Vision Pro, sensors and software monitor head tracking, allowing you to look around inside of immersive content, and your perspective in that experience mirrors your actual head movement (for an added suspension of disbelief).

Home View: The main home screen on Apple Vision Pro. By default, you can see the first page of your apps, but the tab bar on the left lets you change to Environments or to connection with others. To open Home View, press the Digital Crown or say, "Hey Siri, show me Home View."

immersive video: An Apple term for its mixed reality–like video experiences that make viewers feel like they're in another place.

Light Seal: Magnetically secured to the inside of the Apple Vision Pro headset, the Light Seal gently conforms to your face and helps deliver a precise fit while blocking out stray light. It comes in a range of different shapes.

Mac Virtual Display: This technology lets you view your Mac computer's screen on Apple Vision Pro and use your Mac trackpad to share the pointer between your Mac and Apple Vision Pro.

mixed reality (MR): A device that combines virtual reality and augmented reality, a blend of physical and digital worlds. *See also* virtual reality (VR) *and* augmented reality (AR).

MR: *See* mixed reality (MR).

Persona: A digital representation of you, as scanned by the Apple Vision Pro headset, which you use to connect with others online. The headset's cameras capture images and 3D measurements of your face, head, upper body, and facial expressions.

Pro Loop Dual Band: Designed for and included with Apple Vision Pro, the Pro Dual Loop Band features a pair of upper and lower straps for a more precise fit. It attaches to the Audio Straps with a simple and secure mechanism. Release tabs allow you to quickly detach it when needed.

SharePlay: A feature included with many Apple products that enables you to use FaceTime video calls for simultaneous file access or collaboration, such as listening to music together, watching movies, playing games, or working on documents.

Siri: Apple's personal assistant, usually summoned by your voice (saying "Hey Siri"), followed by a question or command. Siri is available across all Apple operating systems: iOS, iPadOS, watchOS, macOS, tvOS, audioOS, and visionOS.

Solo Knit Band: Designed exclusively for Apple Vision Pro, the Solo Knit Band is 3D knitted as a single piece that holds the headset in place and creates a unique rib structure that provides cushioning, breathability, and stretch.

spatial audio: The process of placing different sounds in different locations around the room. For added immersion, filmmakers and sound designers can precisely place individual sounds anywhere around the room to create an all-encompassing soundscape.

spatial computing: Any form of human–computer interaction perceived by users as taking place in the real world around them. *See also* mixed reality (MR).

spatial image: An Apple term for a three-dimensional photo that looks lifelike because of the added depth.

spatial Persona: Appearing like a hologram, your spatial Persona can be seen in supported apps while you're wearing Apple Vision Pro, allowing people to see a digital representation of you while you're engaged in another support app, like Freeform or during a board game. Your spatial Persona allows you to move around, make eye contact, or watch movies together. You can use spatial Personas with up to five participants at once. *See also* Persona *and* SharePlay.

spatial video: An Apple term for a three-dimensional video that looks lifelike because of the added depth.

tab bar: A navigation interface along the left side of several Apple Vision Pro apps that lets you see and select content.

top button: Located above your left eye in Apple Vision Pro, you can press the top button to perform various functions while you're wearing the headset. Its primary purpose is to capture spatial photos and videos. *See also* spatial photo *and* spatial video.

virtual reality (VR): Usually seen while wearing a VR headset, virtual reality is a computer-generated simulation of a three-dimensional environment that you can interact with.

visionOS: Apple's proprietary operating system that runs Apple Vision Pro. visionOS is Apple's first spatial reality or mixed reality operating system. *See also* spatial reality *and* mixed reality (MR).

VR: *See* virtual reality (VR).

ZEISS Optical Inserts: Devices that provide vision correction for people who wear glasses, so they have a better experience while wearing Apple Vision Pro.

Index

H

I

Q

R

S

About the Author

Specializing in consumer electronics, online trends and interactive entertainment, Marc Saltzman is a prolific journalist, author, radio/podcast host, TV personality, and keynote speaker. *Apple Vision Pro For Dummies* is Marc's 17th book since 1996; he is also the author of *Apple Watch For Dummies* and *Siri For Dummies* (both published by Wiley). As a freelance writer, Marc contributes to more than 25 high-profile publications, including *USA Today,* Reviewed.com, *Reader's Digest, AARP,* MSN, Common Sense Media, *Costco Connection,* Postmedia newspapers (like the *National Post* and the *Toronto Sun*), *Zoomer, Homefront* magazine, the *Toronto Star,* and others. Marc hosts the Tech Impact TV show, seen on Bloomberg Television and FOX Business, and has been an on-air contributor to NBC News NOW, CNN, FOX, and *Good Morning America.* In Canada, Marc served as the host of "Gear Guide" (seen at Cineplex movie theaters and sister chains) for 11 years, and currently hosts the Tech Tuesday segment on Global Television. Marc's syndicated radio show, *Tech It Out* (www.marcsaltzman.com/podcasts), can be heard on more than 100 radio stations across the United States every weekend and is also a podcast on popular platforms like Spotify, Apple Podcasts, Amazon's Audible, iHeartRadio, TuneIn, Stitcher, and others.

Follow Marc on X at @marc_saltzman or on Instagram at @marcsaltzman.

Dedication

This book is dedicated to my extraordinary life partner, Kellie, and my three awesome twentysomething kids, Maya, Jacob, and Ethan. I pinch myself every day. Thank you for your love and unwavering support.

Author's Acknowledgments

I'd like to acknowledge all the talented folks at John Wiley & Sons. This book wouldn't have happened without their passion, professionalism, patience, and knowledge. In particular, I'd like to thank my extremely gifted editor, Elizabeth Kuball; technical editor extraordinaire Doug Holland; as well amazing associate editor Elizabeth Stilwell and acquisitions editor Steven Hayes, whom I've had the pleasure of knowing for 15 years.

Publisher's Acknowledgments

Associate Editor: Elizabeth Stilwell

Managing Editor: Kristie Pyles

Editor: Elizabeth Kuball

Technical Editor: Doug Holland

Proofreader: Debbye Butler

Production Editor: Tamilmani Varadharaj

Cover Image: © Ivan Baranov/shutterstock.com

Take dummies with you everywhere you go!

Whether you are excited about e-books, want more from the web, must have your mobile apps, or are swept up in social media, dummies makes everything easier.

Find us online!

dummies.com

Leverage the power

Dummies is the global leader in the reference category and one of the most trusted and highly regarded brands in the world. No longer just focused on books, customers now have access to the dummies content they need in the format they want. Together we'll craft a solution that engages your customers, stands out from the competition, and helps you meet your goals.

Advertising & Sponsorships

Connect with an engaged audience on a powerful multimedia site, and position your message alongside expert how-to content. Dummies.com is a one-stop shop for free, online information and know-how curated by a team of experts.

- Targeted ads
- Video
- Email Marketing
- Microsites
- Sweepstakes sponsorship

20 MILLION PAGE VIEWS **EVERY SINGLE MONTH**

15 MILLION UNIQUE VISITORS PER MONTH

43% OF ALL VISITORS ACCESS THE SITE **VIA THEIR MOBILE DEVICES**

700,000 NEWSLETTER SUBSCRIPTIONS **TO THE INBOXES OF**

300,000 UNIQUE INDIVIDUALS EVERY WEEK

# of dummies

Custom Publishing

Reach a global audience in any language by creating a solution that will differentiate you from competitors, amplify your message, and encourage customers to make a buying decision.

- Apps
- Books
- eBooks
- Video
- Audio
- Webinars

Brand Licensing & Content

Leverage the strength of the world's most popular reference brand to reach new audiences and channels of distribution.

For more information, visit dummies.com/biz

PERSONAL ENRICHMENT

9781119187790
USA $26.00
CAN $31.99
UK £19.99

9781119179030
USA $21.99
CAN $25.99
UK £16.99

9781119293354
USA $24.99
CAN $29.99
UK £17.99

9781119293347
USA $22.99
CAN $27.99
UK £16.99

9781119310068
USA $22.99
CAN $27.99
UK £16.99

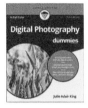

9781119235606
USA $24.99
CAN $29.99
UK £17.99

9781119251163
USA $24.99
CAN $29.99
UK £17.99

9781119235491
USA $26.99
CAN $31.99
UK £19.99

9781119279952
USA $24.99
CAN $29.99
UK £17.99

9781119283133
USA $24.99
CAN $29.99
UK £17.99

9781119287117
USA $24.99
CAN $29.99
UK £16.99

9781119130246
USA $22.99
CAN $27.99
UK £16.99

PROFESSIONAL DEVELOPMENT

9781119311041
USA $24.99
CAN $29.99
UK £17.99

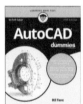

9781119255796
USA $39.99
CAN $47.99
UK £27.99

9781119293439
USA $26.99
CAN $31.99
UK £19.99

9781119281467
USA $26.99
CAN $31.99
UK £19.99

9781119280651
USA $29.99
CAN $35.99
UK £21.99

9781119251132
USA $24.99
CAN $29.99
UK £17.99

9781119310563
USA $34.00
CAN $41.99
UK £24.99

9781119181705
USA $29.99
CAN $35.99
UK £21.99

9781119263593
USA $26.99
CAN $31.99
UK £19.99

9781119257769
USA $29.99
CAN $35.99
UK £21.99

9781119293477
USA $26.99
CAN $31.99
UK £19.99

9781119265313
USA $24.99
CAN $29.99
UK £17.99

9781119239314
USA $29.99
CAN $35.99
UK £21.99

9781119293323
USA $29.99
CAN $35.99
UK £21.99

dummies.com

dummies®
A Wiley Brand

Learning Made Easy

ACADEMIC

9781119293576
USA $19.99
CAN $23.99
UK £15.99

9781119293637
USA $19.99
CAN $23.99
UK £15.99

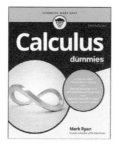

9781119293491
USA $19.99
CAN $23.99
UK £15.99

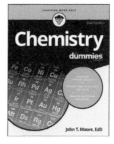

9781119293460
USA $19.99
CAN $23.99
UK £15.99

9781119293590
USA $19.99
CAN $23.99
UK £15.99

9781119215844
USA $26.99
CAN $31.99
UK £19.99

9781119293378
USA $22.99
CAN $27.99
UK £16.99

9781119293521
USA $19.99
CAN $23.99
UK £15.99

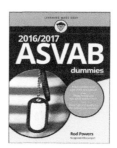

9781119239178
USA $18.99
CAN $22.99
UK £14.99

9781119263883
USA $26.99
CAN $31.99
UK £19.99

Available Everywhere Books Are Sold

dummies.com